Other Books by James Montgomery Boice

Witness and Revelation in the Gospel of John
Philippians: An Expositional Commentary
The Sermon on the Mount
How to Really Live It Up
The Last and Future World
How God Can Use Nobodies
The Gospel of John: An Expositional Commentary (5 vols.)
"Galatians" in the *Expositor's Bible Commentary*
Can You Run Away from God?
Our Sovereign God, editor
God the Redeemer (Volume II of this series)

Foundations of the Christian Faith
VOLUME I

THE
SOVEREIGN GOD

James Montgomery Boice

InterVarsity Press
Downers Grove
Illinois 60515

InterVarsity Press is the book publishing division
of Inter-Varsity Christian Fellowship,
a student movement active on campus at hundreds
of universities, colleges and schools of nursing.
For information about local and regional
activities, write IVCF, 233 Langdon St.,
Madison, WI 53703.

Biblical quotations, unless otherwise noted,
are from the Revised Standard Version of the Bible,
copyrighted 1946, 1952, © 1971, 1973, and are
used by permission.

ISBN 0-87784-743-6

Library of Congress Catalog Card
Number: 77-014879

Printed in the United States of America

To him
whom to know is
life eternal

Preface

Shortly after Harvard College was founded in 1636, the trustees of the school wrote, "Let every student be plainly instructed, and earnestly pressed to consider well [that the] maine end of his life and studies is to know God and Jesus Christ ... and therefore to lay Christ in the bottome, as the only foundation of all sound knowledge and learning." In the 340 years since, Harvard (as well as most other schools, colleges and universities) has moved far in a purely secular direction. But the words of those early trustees are still true, and many people still see their chief goal in life as knowing God better.

It is for such people that this book has been written.

Not often do I, as an author, sense an area in which no book seems to exist and for which one should be written. But the area covered by this book and the three other volumes of this series is an exception, in my judgment. For years I have looked for a work that could be given to a person (particularly a new Christian) who is alert and questioning and who could profit from a comprehensive but readable overview of the

Christian faith, a basic theology from A to Z. But I could not find anything that was quite what I had in mind and, thus, determined that I should attempt to write it myself.

It is impossible for anyone to do something of this scope perfectly, of course. So I delayed beginning my work for several years. I could have delayed indefinitely. A time comes, however, when regardless of limitations one should simply go ahead and do the best one can. The result has been a projected series of four volumes, corresponding more or less to the ground covered by John Calvin in the four books of his monumental *Institutes of the Christian Religion.*

This book is not a rehash of the *Institutes,* although I am greatly indebted to Calvin and although the theology of this volume is Calvinistic. Rather, it is an attempt (a) to cover the same ground in highly readable language yet at the same time (b) to introduce themes which Calvin did not treat but which call for treatment today and (c) to seek to relate all doctrine to contemporary rather than ancient views and problems. This volume deals with the doctrine of God. The other volumes deal with (1) sin and the redemptive work of Christ, (2) the Holy Spirit and the application of redemption to the individual and (3) the church and the meaning of history.

I am indebted to a number of other writers and thinkers, as the footnotes indicate. Among them are men whom I have come to know and with whom I have worked as a result of the annual Philadelphia Conference on Reformed Theology, founded in 1974—John R. W. Stott, J. I. Packer, R. C. Sproul, Ralph Keiper and Roger Nicole. I am also indebted to (and frequently quote from) Thomas Watson, B. B. Warfield, R. A. Torrey, A. W. Tozer, A. W. Pink, C. S. Lewis, Emil Brunner, F. F. Bruce, Clark Pinnock, John Warwick Montgomery, Francis A. Schaeffer and others.

A portion of this material has already appeared in an article entitled "New Vistas in Historical Jesus Research," *Christianity Today* (March 14, 1968). Other parts are similar to portions of my other writings, particularly the material on Scripture which appears in _The Gospel of John,_ Vol. 2, chapters 12—15. Other material in this book has already appeared in a shortened version in the June-August 1976 and June 1977 issues of _Bible Study Magazine._

I wish to express my appreciation to Miss Caecilie M. Foelster, my secretary, who works with me on all my books, seeing them through the various stages of production. Also, I am thankful to the evening congregation of Tenth Presbyterian Church in Philadelphia to whom these chapters were first presented in sermon form. The congregation sustained and encouraged me, and it was a joy to preach these themes to them.

May God be honored by the publication and reading of this book. I pray that many might be quickened in their desire to know God better and might actually come to know him better as a result of it.

PART I
THE KNOWLEDGE OF GOD

*The fear of the LORD is the beginning of
wisdom, and the knowledge of the Holy One is
insight. (Prov. 9:10)*

*And this is eternal life, that they know thee the
only true God, and Jesus Christ whom
thou hast sent. (Jn. 17:3)*

*For the wrath of God is revealed from heaven
against all ungodliness and wickedness
of men who by their wickedness suppress the
truth. For what can be known about
God is plain to them, because God has shown it
to them. Ever since the creation of the
world his invisible nature, namely, his eternal
power and deity, has been clearly perceived
in the things that have been made. So
they are without excuse; for although they
knew God they did not honor him as
God or give thanks to him, but they became
futile in their thinking and their
senseless minds were darkened. Claiming to be
wise, they became fools, and exchanged
the glory of the immortal God for images
resembling mortal man or birds or animals or
reptiles. (Rom. 1:18-23)*

1

ON KNOWING GOD

One hot night in the early years of the Christian era a sophisticated and highly educated man named Nicodemus came to see a young rabbi, Jesus of Nazareth. The man wanted to discuss reality. So he began the conversation with a statement of where his own personal search for truth had taken him. He said, "Rabbi, we know that you are a teacher come from God; for no one can do these signs that you do, unless God is with him" (Jn. 3:2).

With the exception of the word *Rabbi*, which was merely a polite form of address, the first words were a claim to considerable knowledge. Nicodemus said, "We know." Then he began to rehearse the things he knew (or thought he knew) and with which he wanted to begin the discussion: (1) that Jesus was continuing to do many miracles; (2) that these miracles were intended to authenticate him as a teacher sent from God; and that, therefore, (3) Jesus was one to whom he should listen. Unfortunately for Nicodemus, Jesus replied that such an approach to knowledge was wrong and that Nicodemus could therefore know nothing until he had first experienced an inward, spiritual transformation. "You must be born anew," Jesus told him (Jn. 3:7).

Nicodemus's subsequent remarks showed at least an implicit recognition of his lack of knowledge in important things. For he began to ask questions, "How can a man be born when he is old? How can this be?" (vv. 4, 9). Jesus taught him that true knowledge begins with spiritual knowledge, knowledge of God, and that this is to be found in God's revelation of himself in the Bible and in Jesus' own life and work, the work of the Savior.

Contemporary Crisis

This ancient conversation is relevant to our day. For the problems and frustrations that Nicodemus faced nearly two thousand years ago are with us in our time also. Nicodemus possessed knowledge, but he lacked the key to that knowledge, the element that would put it all together. He knew certain things, but his search for truth had brought him to the point of personal crisis. That sounds familiar. Much is known in our time. In the sense of information or technical knowledge, more is known today than at any previous time in history. Yet the kind of knowledge that integrates information and thereby gives meaning to life is strangely absent.

The nature of the problem can be seen by examining the two almost exclusive approaches to knowledge today. On the one hand there is the idea that reality can be known *by reason alone*. That approach is not new, of course. It is the approach developed by Plato and therefore assumed by much of the Greek and Roman thought after him. In Plato's philosophy, knowledge became knowledge of the eternal and unalterable essence of things, not merely knowledge of changeable phenomena. That is, it was a knowledge of forms, ideas or ideals. Our nearest equivalent would be the so-called laws of science.

On the surface, this approach to knowledge through the exercise of supposedly impartial reason seems desirable, for it is productive—as the technical advances of our day often indicate. But it is not without problems. For one thing, it is highly impersonal knowledge and, as some would say, highly depersonalizing. In this approach reality becomes a thing (an equation, law or, worse yet, mere data), and men and women become things also, with the inevitable result that they may therefore be manipulated like any other raw material for whatever ends.

An example is the manipulation of poorer nations by rich nations for the sake of the rich nation's expanding economy, that is, the injustice analyzed and rightly condemned by Karl Marx in *The Communist Manifesto, Capital* and other writings. Another example is that of communism itself which, in spite of its desire to better the lot of the masses, actually manipulates them for ideological ends. On the personal level there is the science of behavioral technology and the frightening teaching of a man like B. F. Skinner of Harvard University who claims that individuals must be conditioned scientifically for the good of society.

There is also another problem with the attempt to know reality through reason alone. The approach does not give an adequate basis for ethics. It can tell us what *is*, but it cannot tell us what ought to be. Consequently, the extraordinary technical advances of our time are accompanied by an extreme and debilitating moral permissiveness which promises in time to break down even the values and system that made both the advances and the permissiveness possible. Interestingly, the same thing was also true of the Greek philosophers, who, although they were men of great intellect, on occasion led depraved lives.

In recent years the failures of the rationalistic system have impressed themselves on a new generation with the result that many in the Western world have abandoned reason in order to seek reality *through emotional experience.* In the ancient world, in reaction to the impersonality of Greek philosophy, this was done through intense participation in the rites of the mystery religions. These promised an emotional union with some god, induced by lighting, music, incense or perhaps by drugs. In our time the same approach is surfacing through the drug cult, rediscovery of the Eastern religions, Transcendental Meditation and other supposedly "mind-expanding" practices.

This modern approach also has several problems. First, the experience does not last. It is transient. Each attempt to achieve reality through emotional experience promises some sort of "high." But the "high" is inevitably followed by a "low," with the additional problem that increasingly intense stimuli seem to be necessary to repeat the experience. Eventually this ends either in self-destruction or acute disillusionment. A second problem is that the approach to reality through emotion does not satisfy the mind. Promoters of these experiences, particularly drug experiences, speak of a more intense perception of reality that results from them. But their experience has no rational content. The part of the human being that wants to think about such things and understand them is unsatisfied.

The result of this situation is a crisis in the area of knowledge today, as in ancient times. Many thinking people quite honestly do not know where to turn. The rationalistic approach is impersonal and amoral. The emotionalistic approach is without content, transient, and also often immoral. "Is this the end?" many are asking. "Are there no other possibilities? Is there not a third way?"

A Third Way
At this point Christianity comes forward with the claim that there is a third way and that this way is strong at precisely those points where the other approaches are lacking. The

basis of this third approach is that there is a God who has created all things and who himself gives his creation meaning. Further, we can know him. This is an exciting and satisfying possibility. It is exciting because it involves the possibility of contact between the individual and God, however insignificant the individual may appear in his or her own eyes or in the eyes of others. It is satisfying because it is knowledge not of an idea or thing but of a supremely personal Being, and because it issues in a profound change of conduct.

This is what the Bible means when it says, "The fear of the LORD is the beginning of knowledge" (Prov. 1:7). And, "The fear of the LORD is the beginning of wisdom, and the knowledge of the Holy One is insight" (Prov. 9:10).

Here, however, we must be clear about what we mean when we speak of "knowing God," for many common uses of the word *know* are inadequate to convey the biblical understanding. There is a use of the word *know* by which we mean "awareness." In this sense we say that we know where somebody lives or that we know that certain events are transpiring somewhere in the world. It is a kind of knowledge, but it does not involve us personally. It has little bearing on our lives. This is not what the Bible means when it speaks of knowing God.

Another use of the word *know* means "knowing about" something or someone. It is knowledge by description. For instance, we may say that we know New York City or London or Moscow. By that we mean that we are aware of the geographic layout of the city, we know the names of the streets, where the major stores are and other facts. We may have gained our knowledge of the city by actually living there. But it is also possible that we may have gained our knowledge by reading books. In the religious realm this type of knowledge would apply to theology which, although important, is not the whole or even the heart of religion. The Bible tells us much about God that we should know. (In fact, much of what follows in this book is directed to our need for such knowledge.)

But this is not enough. Even the greatest theologians can be confused and can find life meaningless.

True knowledge of God is also more than *knowledge by experience*. To go back to the earlier example, it would be possible for someone who has lived in a particular city to say, "But my knowledge is *not* book knowledge. I have actually lived there. I have walked the streets, shopped in the stores, attended the theaters. I have experienced the city. I really know it." To this we would have to reply that the knowledge involved is certainly a step beyond anything we have talked about thus far, but still it is not the full idea of knowledge in the Christian sense.

Suppose, for instance, that a person should go out into a starlit field in the cool of a summer evening and gaze up into the twinkling heavens and come away with the claim that in that field he has come to know God. What do we say to such a person? The Christian does not have to deny the validity of that experience, up to a point. It is certainly a richer knowledge than mere awareness of God ("There is a God") or mere knowledge about him ("God is powerful and is the Creator of all that we see and know"). Still, the Christian insists, this is less than what the Bible means by true knowledge. For when the Bible speaks of knowing God it means being made alive by God in a new sense (being "born again"), conversing with God (so that he becomes more than some great "Something" out there, so that he becomes a friend), and being profoundly changed in the process.

All this is leading us, step by step, to a better understanding of the word *knowledge*. But still another qualification is needed. According to the Bible even when the highest possible meaning is given to the word *know*, knowing God is still not merely knowing *God*. For it is never *knowing God in isolation*. It is always knowing God in his relationship to us. Consequently, according to the Bible, knowledge of God takes place only where there is also knowledge of ourselves in our deep spiritual need and where there is an accompanying acceptance of God's gracious provision for our need through the work of Christ and the application of that work to us by God's Spirit. Knowledge of God takes place in the context of Christian piety, worship and devotion. The Bible teaches that this knowledge of God takes place (where it does take place), not so much because we search after God—because we do not —but because God reveals himself to us in Christ and in the Scriptures.

J. I. Packer writes of this knowledge, "Knowing God involves, first, listening to God's word and receiving it as the Holy Spirit interprets it, in application to oneself; second, noting God's nature and character, as His word and works reveal it; third, accepting His invitations, and doing what He commands; fourth, recognising, and rejoicing in, the love that He has shown in thus approaching one and drawing one into this divine fellowship."[1]

Why Bother?

"But just a minute," someone might argue. "All that sounds complicated and difficult. In fact, it seems too difficult. If that's what is involved, I want no part of it. Give me one good reason why I should bother." That is a fair objection, but there is an adequate answer to it. In fact, there are several.

First, knowledge of God is important, for only through the knowledge of God can an individual enter into what the Bible terms *eternal life*. Jesus indicated this when he prayed, "And this is eternal life, that they know thee the only true God, and Jesus Christ whom thou hast sent" (Jn. 17:3). At first glance even this does not seem important enough to the "natural man" to make him want to know God at all costs. But this is because, lacking eternal life, he cannot begin to understand what he is missing. He is like a person who says that he does not appreciate good music. His dislike does not make the music worthless; it simply indicates an inadequate grounds of appreciation in him. So also those who do not appreciate God's offer of life indicate that they do not have the capability of understanding or valuing what they are lacking. The Bible says, "The unspiritual man does not receive the gifts of the Spirit of God, for they are folly to him, and he is not able to understand them because they are spiritually discerned" (1 Cor. 2:14).

It might help such a person to be told that the promise of eternal life is also the promise of being able to live life fully as an authentic human being. This is true, but it is also true that eternal life means more than this. It means coming alive, not only in a new but also in an eternal sense. It is what Jesus meant when he said, "I am the resurrection and the life; he who believes in me, though he die, yet shall he live, and whoever lives and believes in me shall never die" (Jn. 11:25-26).

Second, knowledge of God is important because, as pointed out earlier, it also involves *knowledge of ourselves*. Our day is the day of the psychiatrist and psychologist. Men and women spend billions of dollars annually in an attempt to know themselves, to sort out their psyches. Certainly there is need for psychiatry, particularly Christian psychiatry. But this alone is inadequate in the ultimate sense if it does not bring individuals into a knowledge of God against which their own worth and failures may be estimated.

On the one hand, knowledge of ourselves through the knowledge of God is humbling. We are not God nor are we like him. He is holy; we are unholy. He is good; we are not good. He is wise; we are foolish. He is strong; we are weak. He is loving and gracious; we are filled with hate and with selfish affections. Therefore, to know God is to see ourselves as Isaiah did: "Woe is me! For I am lost; for I am a man of unclean lips, and I dwell in the midst of a people of unclean lips; for my eyes have seen the King, the LORD of hosts!" (Is. 6:5). Or as Peter did: "Depart from me, for I am a sinful man, O Lord" (Lk. 5:8). On the other hand, such knowledge of ourselves through the knowledge of God is also reassuring and satisfying. For in spite of what we have become we are still God's creation and are loved by him. No higher dignity has been given to women and men than the dignity the Bible gives them.

Third, the knowledge of God also gives us _knowledge of this world:_ its good and its evil, its past and its future, its purpose and its impending judgment at the hand of God. In one sense, this is an extension of the point just made. If knowledge of God gives us knowledge of ourselves, it also inevitably gives us knowledge of the world; for the world is mostly the individuals who compose it written large. On the other hand the world stands in a special relationship to God, in its sin and rebellion as well as in its value as a vehicle for his purposes. It is a confusing place until we know the God who made it and learn from him why he made it and what is to happen to it.

A fourth reason the knowledge of God is important is that it is the only way to _personal holiness_. This is a goal that the natural man hardly desires. But it is essential nonetheless. Our problems derive not only from the fact that we are ignorant of God but also from the fact that we are sinful. We do not want the good. At times we hate it, even when the good is to our benefit.

The knowledge of God leads to holiness. To know God as he is, is to love him as he is and to want to be like him. This is the message of one of the Bible's most important verses about the knowledge of God. Jeremiah, the ancient prophet of Israel, wrote, "Let not the wise man glory in his wisdom, let not the mighty man glory in his might, let not the rich man glory in his riches; but let him who glories glory in this, that he understands and knows me, that I am the LORD who practice steadfast love, justice, and righteousness in the earth; for in these things I delight, says the LORD" (Jer. 9: 23-24). Jeremiah also wrote about a day when those who don't know God will come to know him. "And no longer shall each man teach his neighbor and each his brother, saying, 'Know the LORD,' for they shall all know me, from the least of them to the greatest, says the LORD; for I will forgive their iniquity, and I will remember their sin no more" (Jer. 31:34).

Finally, the knowledge of God is important in that it is only through a knowledge of God that *the church and those who compose it can become strong.* In ourselves we are weak, but as Daniel wrote, "The people who know their God shall stand firm and take action" (Dan. 11:32).

We do not have a strong church today, nor do we have many strong Christians. We can trace the cause to an acute lack of sound spiritual knowledge. Why is the church weak? Why are individual Christians weak? It is because they have allowed their minds to become conformed to the "spirit of this age," with its mechanistic, godless thinking. They have forgotten what God is like and what he promises to do for those who trust him. Ask an average Christian to talk about God. After getting past the expected answers you will find that his god is a little god of vacillating sentiments. He is a god who would like to save the world, but who cannot. He would like to restrain evil, but somehow he finds it beyond his power. So he has withdrawn into semiretirement, being willing to give good advice in a grandfatherly sort of way, but for the most part he has left his children to fend for themselves in a dangerous environment.

Such a god is not the God of the Bible. Those who know their God perceive the error in that kind of thinking and act accordingly. The God of the Bible is not weak; he is strong. He is all-mighty. Nothing happens without his permission or apart from his purposes—even evil. Nothing disturbs or puzzles him. His purposes are always accomplished. Therefore, those who know him rightly act with boldness, assured that God is with them to accomplish his own desirable purposes in their lives.

Do we need an example? We can find no better one than

Daniel. Daniel and his friends were godly men in the godless environment of ancient Babylon. They were slaves, good slaves. They served the court. But difficulty arose when they refused to obey anything in opposition to the commands of the true God whom they knew and worshiped. When Nebuchadnezzar's great statue was set up and all were required to fall down and worship it, Daniel and his friends refused. When prayer to anyone but King Darius was banned for thirty days, Daniel did as he always did: he prayed to God three times a day before an open window.

What was wrong with these men? Had they fooled themselves about the consequences? Did they think that their failure to comply would go unseen? Not at all. They knew the consequences, but they also knew God. They were able to be strong, trusting God to have his way with them whether it meant salvation or destruction in the lions' den or the furnace. These men said, "If it be so, our God whom we serve is able to deliver us from the burning fiery furnace; and he will deliver us out of your hand, O king. But if not, be it known to you, O king, that we will not serve your gods or worship the golden image which you have set up" (Dan. 3:17-18).

A weak god produces no strong men, nor does he deserve to be worshiped. A strong God, the God of the Bible, is a source of strength to those who know him.

The Highest Science

So let us learn about God and come to know God in the fullest, biblical sense. Jesus encouraged us to do this when he said, "Come to me, all who labor and are heavy laden, and I will give you rest. Take my yoke upon you, and learn from me; for I am gentle and lowly in heart, and you will find rest for your souls" (Mt. 11:28-29). This is true wisdom for everyone. It is the special duty and privilege of the Christian.

What is the proper course of study for one who is a child of God? Is it not God himself? There are other worthwhile areas of learning, it is true. But the highest science, the most mind-expanding area of all, is the Godhead. Spurgeon once wrote:

There is something exceedingly improving to the mind in a contemplation of the Divinity. It is a subject so vast, that all our thoughts are lost in its immensity; so deep, that our pride is drowned in its infinity. Other subjects we can comprehend and grapple with; in them we feel a kind of self-content, and go on our way with the thought, "Behold I am wise." But when we come to this master-science, finding that our plumb-line cannot sound its depth, and that our eagle eye cannot see its height, we turn away with the . . . solemn exclamation, "I am but of yesterday and know nothing." . . . But while the subject humbles the mind, it also expands it. . . . Nothing will so enlarge the intellect, nothing so magnify the whole soul of man, as a devout, earnest, continuing investigation of the great subject of the Deity. [2]

Every Christian should confidently pursue this goal. God has promised that those who seek him will find him. To those who knock, the door shall be opened.

2 THE UNKNOWN GOD

"Nearly all the wisdom we possess, that is to say, true and sound wisdom, consists of two parts: the knowledge of God and of ourselves."[1] These words from the opening paragraph of John Calvin's *Institutes of the Christian Religion* mark the point to which the preceding chapter has brought us, but they also introduce a new problem. If it is true that wisdom consists in the "knowledge of God and of ourselves," we are at once led to ask, "But who has such knowledge? Who truly knows God or knows himself?" If we are honest, we must admit that as long as we are left to ourselves and our own abilities, the only possible answer is "No one." Left to ourselves, not one of us truly knows God. Nor do we know ourselves adequately.

What is the trouble? Clearly, we do not know ourselves because we have first failed to know God. But why don't we know God? Is he unknowable? Is the fault his or is it ours? Obviously, it is more appealing to us to blame God. But before we jump to that conclusion we should be conscious of what is involved. If the fault is ours, although that fact in itself may be uncomfortable, then at least it can be corrected, for God can do anything. He can intervene. On the other hand, if the fault is God's (or, as we might prefer to say, if the fault is in the very nature of things), then nothing at all can be done. The key to knowledge will inevitably elude us, and life is absurd.

In *The Dust of Death* Os Guinness makes this point by describing a comedy skit performed by the German comedian Karl Vallentin. In this routine the comic comes onto a stage illuminated only by one small circle of light. He paces around and around this circle with a worried face. He is searching for something. After awhile a policeman joins him and asks what he has lost. "I've lost the key to my house," Vallentin answers. The policeman joins the hunt, but the search eventually appears useless.

"Are you sure you lost it here?" asks the policeman.

"Oh no!" says Vallentin, pointing to a dark corner. "It was over there."

"Then why are you looking here?"

"There's no light over there," answers the comic.[2]

If there is no God or if there is a God but the failure to know him is God's fault, then the search for knowledge is like the search of the German comedian. Where the search should be made, there is no light; and where there is light there is no point in searching. But is this the case? The Bible declares that the problem is not God's but ours. Therefore, the problem is solvable. It is solvable because God can take, and actually has taken, steps to reveal himself to us, thereby providing us with the missing key to knowledge.

Awareness of God
We must begin with the problem, however: strange as it may sound, the person who does not know God, still in some lesser but valid sense, does know him yet represses that knowledge.

Here we must go back to the distinction between an "awareness" of God and truly "knowing God." Knowing God is entering into a knowledge of our deep spiritual need and of God's provision for that need, and then coming to trust and reverence God. Awareness of God is merely the sense that there is a God and that he deserves to be obeyed and worshiped. Men and women do not naturally know, obey or worship God. But they do have an awareness of him.

This brings us to some of the most important words ever recorded for the benefit of humanity—from the apostle Paul's letter to the newly established church in Rome. They contain the apostle's first thesis in his greatest exposition of Christian doctrine.

> *For the wrath of God is revealed from heaven against all ungodliness and wickedness of men who by their wickedness suppress the truth. For what can be known about God is plain to them, because God has shown it to them. Ever since the creation of the world his invisible nature, namely, his eternal power and deity, has been clearly perceived in the things that have been made. So they are without excuse; for although they knew God they did not honor him as God or give thanks to him, but they became futile in their thinking and their senseless minds were darkened. Claiming to be wise, they became fools, and exchanged the glory of the immortal God for images resembling mortal man or birds or animals or reptiles. (Rom. 1:18-23)*

Here we see three important ideas. First, the wrath of God is displayed against the natural man. Second, man has willfully rejected God. Third, this rejection has taken place in spite of a natural awareness of God possessed by each person.

Double Revelation
The third point, the natural awareness of God possessed by every person, is the necessary place to begin. For here we see that, although no one naturally knows God, the failure we have in knowing God is not God's fault. God has given us a twofold revelation of himself, and we all have this revelation.

The first part is the *revelation of God in nature*. Paul's argument may be rephrased as saying that all that can be known about God by the natural man has been revealed in nature. Of course we must acknowledge that this is limited knowledge. In fact, Paul defines it as just two things: God's eternal power and his deity. But although such knowledge is limited, it is sufficient to remove excuse if any person fails to move on from it to seek God fully. In contemporary speech the phrase "eternal power" could be reduced to the word *supremeness*, and "deity" could be changed to *being*. Paul is saying then that there is ample and entirely convincing evidence in nature of a Supreme Being. God exists, and human beings know it. That is the argument. When men and women subsequently refuse to acknowledge and worship God, as they do, the fault is not in a lack of evidence but in their irrational and resolute determination not to know him.

The Old Testament speaks of the clear revelation of God in nature. "The heavens are telling the glory of God; and the firmament proclaims his handiwork. Day to day pours forth speech, and night to night declares knowledge. There is no speech, nor are there words; their voice is not heard; yet their voice goes out through all the earth, and their words to the end of the world" (Ps. 19:1-4). The point is that the revelation of God in nature is sufficient to convince anyone of God's existence and power, if the individual will have it.

There is a second part to God's self-revelation. We might call it an *internal revelation* or, at least, the internal capacity for receiving one. No one in his or her natural state has actually come to know God in the full biblical sense. But each person has been given the capacity for receiving the natural revelation. Paul is talking about this capacity when he says that "what can be known about God is plain *to them*" (Rom. 1:19).

Suppose that you are driving down the street and come to a sign that says, "Detour—Turn Left." But you ignore this and drive on. It happens that there is a police officer present, who then stops you and begins to write out a ticket. What excuse might you have? You can argue that you didn't see the sign. But that makes no difference. As long as you are driving the car, the responsibility for seeing the sign and obeying it is yours. Further, you are responsible if, having ignored the sign, you recklessly plunge on over a cliff and destroy both yourself and your passengers.

Paul is saying, first, there is a sign. It is the revelation of God in nature. Second, you have "vision." If you choose to ignore the sign, and so court disaster, the guilt is your own. In fact, the judgment of God (like that of the police officer) comes, not because you didn't or couldn't know God, but because being aware of God you nevertheless refused to acknowledge him as God. Paul writes, "So they are without excuse; for although they knew God they did not honor him as God or give thanks to him" (Rom. 1:20-21).

Paul is not saying that there is enough evidence about God in nature so that the scientist, who carefully probes nature's mysteries, can be aware of him. He is not saying that the sign is there but hidden, that we are only able to find it if we look carefully. Paul is saying that the sign is plain. It is a billboard. No one, no matter how weak-minded or insignificant, can be excused for missing it. There is enough evidence of God in a flower to lead a child as well as a scientist to worship him. There is sufficient evidence in a tree, a pebble, a grain of sand, a fingerprint, to make us glorify God and thank him. This is the way to knowledge. But people will not do this. They substitute nature or parts of nature for God and find their hearts darkened.

Calvin gives this conclusion. "But although we lack the natural ability to mount up unto the pure and clear knowledge of God, all excuse is cut off because the fault of dullness is within us. And, indeed, we are not allowed thus to pretend ignorance without our conscience itself always convicting us of both baseness and ingratitude."[3]

Rejection of God

When Calvin speaks of baseness and ingratitude he brings us to the second point of Paul's argument in Romans: the fact that all have rejected God in spite of God's revelation of himself in nature. However, in developing this point in Romans (v. 18) Paul also shows the nature of our rejection and why it has taken place.

The key to this universal rejection of God is found in the phrase "who by their wickedness suppress the truth." In Greek the word translated "suppress" is *katechein,* which means "hold," "hold fast," "keep," "take," "hold back," "restrain" or "repress." In a positive sense the word is used to mean holding to whatever is good. Paul speaks of "holding fast the word of life" (Phil. 2:16). In a negative sense it is used to mean wrongly suppressing something or holding it down. Thus the newer translations of the Bible speak in Romans 1:18 of those who "suppress the truth by their wickedness" (NIV), "suppress the truth in unrighteousness" (NASB), and "keep truth imprisoned in their wickedness" (JB). The New English Bible says that such people are "stifling" the truth. This, then, is the nature of the problem. The wrath of God is revealed from heaven against human beings, not because they have simply and perhaps carelessly overlooked the truth, but rather because they have deliberately and wickedly repressed whatever, deep in their hearts, they know about God.

R. C. Sproul has called this argument "the heart of Paul's psychology of atheism,"[4] pointing out it is here that human guilt lies. Sufficient knowledge has been given to all people to cause them to turn from themselves and their own way of life to God and so at least to begin to seek him. But this knowledge, like a great spring, has been pressed down. Now the spring threatens to leap up and demolish the views and lifestyle of the one repressing it. So that person holds it down, suppressing the truth.

Why do we do this? If it is true, as pointed out in the last chapter, that the knowledge of God leads to our chief good and if, as we have just said, the beginning of that knowledge is already present to us, then why do we repress it? Wouldn't we welcome such truth and seek to draw it out? Are people simply irrational at this point? Or is Paul's view faulty?

Paul is not wrong. Men and women do suppress truth. But their reason for doing so is that _they do not like the truth about God._ They don't like the God to which the truth leads them.

Notice that Paul begins these verses from Romans by saying that the wrath of God is revealed from heaven against all "ungodliness and wickedness of men." _Ungodliness_ has a variety of meanings. Here the meaning is not so much that human beings are not like God (though that is true) but that in addition they are in a state of opposition to God in his godly nature. God is sovereign, but people do not like his sovereignty. They do not want to acknowledge that there is One who rightly exercises rule over them. God is holy, but men and women do not like his holiness. His holiness calls our own sinfulness into question. God is all-knowing, but we do not like his knowledge. We do not like a God who sees into the dark recesses of our hearts and knows us intimately. Nearly everything that can be known about God is repugnant to the natural man in one way or another. So he represses the evidence that would lead him in the direction of a true knowledge of God.

The second word is "wickedness." Everything about God is repugnant to the natural man, but the dominant cause of this repugnance is God's righteousness. God is holy, but people are unholy. People are unrighteous, and they like their unrighteousness. Consequently they do not wish to know a God who would press moral claims upon them. To know God would require change. In other words, the refusal to know God is based not so much on intellectual causes as on moral ones.

Substitute Gods

At this point we have come to the true source of the human

problem. Men and women have rejected the beginnings of the knowledge of God for moral and psychological reasons. But they find it impossible to stop there. They have rejected God; but they are still God's creatures and have a need for God (or something like him) in their intellectual and moral make-up. Being unwilling to know the true God and being unable to do without him, they invent substitute gods to take his place. These gods may be the sophisticated scientific laws of our culture, the gods and goddesses of the Greek and Roman worlds or the depraved, bestial images of paganism.

The universality of religion on this planet is not due to men and women being seekers after God, as some have argued. Rather it is because they will not have God yet need something to take God's place.

The process of rejection is a three-stage process well known to contemporary psychologists: trauma, repression and substitution. In his analysis of atheism, Sproul shows that confrontation with the true God shocks and injures people. It is traumatic. Consequently, we repress what we know. "There is no trauma if the eyes are forever closed so that no light penetrates. But the eyes close in reaction to the shock of the light—after the pain has been experienced."[5] The important point here is that the knowledge of God, though repressed, is not destroyed. It remains intact, though deeply buried in the subconscious. The lack is therefore felt, and substitution of "that which is not God" for the true God follows.

God's Wrath

At last, then, we arrive at Paul's first statement, having taken the three main points of the passage in reverse order: the wrath of God is justly revealed against human beings because they suppressed the knowledge of God that was plain to them.

Some people are deeply disturbed by the teaching that the great God of the universe expresses wrath. They understand that God is a God of love, as indeed he is, and cannot see how

God can possess the one characteristic as well as the other. In this they fail either to understand or to know God. A God who does not have wrath against sin is a deformed or crippled God. He lacks something. God is perfect in his love. That is true. But God is also perfect in his wrath which, as Paul tells us in Romans, is "revealed from heaven against all ungodliness and wickedness of men."

In any logical presentation of doctrine, the wrath of God is the first truth we have to learn about him. Why didn't Paul begin by saying that the love of God is revealed from heaven? It is not that God is not love, for he is, as Paul will show later. Rather, it is so we will recognize our deep spiritual need and be prepared to receive the knowledge of God in the Lord Jesus Christ, the Savior, where alone we can receive it. If men and women come to God boasting of their alleged spiritual knowledge, God will declare them to be ignorant. If they come to God boasting of their own achievements, God cannot and will not receive them. But if they come humbly, recognizing that they indeed have rejected what has been clearly revealed about God in nature, that they are without excuse, that God's wrath justly hangs over them, then God will work in their lives. He will show that he has already made a way for removing the wrath due them, that Jesus has borne it, and that the way is now open for their growth in both the love and knowledge of God which is salvation.

PART II
THE WORD OF GOD

All scripture is inspired by God and profitable for teaching, for reproof, for correction, and for training in righteousness, that the man of God may be complete, equipped for every good work. (2 Tim. 3:16-17)

They said to each other, "Did not our hearts burn within us while he talked to us on the road, while he opened to us the scriptures?" (Lk. 24:32)

The law of the LORD is perfect, reviving the soul; the testimony of the LORD is sure, making wise the simple; the precepts of the LORD are right, rejoicing the heart; the commandment of the LORD is pure, enlightening the eyes. (Ps. 19:7-8)

"I say to you, till heaven and earth pass away, not an iota, not a dot, will pass from the law until all is accomplished." (Mt. 5:18)

For the time is coming when people will not endure sound teaching, but having itching ears they will accumulate for themselves teachers to suit their own likings, and will turn away from listening to the truth and wander into myths. (2 Tim. 4:3-4)

Do your best to present yourself to God as one approved, a workman who has no need to be ashamed, rightly handling the word of truth. (2 Tim. 2:15)

3 THE BIBLE

Our study of Christian doctrine has brought us to three great truths: first, the knowledge of God is our chief good; second, God has revealed in nature certain truths about himself to everyone; but third, people have rejected this revelation and have substituted false gods in place of the Creator. Awareness of the true God is conveyed to us externally, in all that we see, and internally through the workings of our own minds and hearts. But we have denied our awareness of God, changing the knowledge we do have into superstition. As a result, the world, for all its wisdom, does not know God and so lacks knowledge of itself also.

What is to be done? It is obvious from what has already been said that men and women can do nothing themselves. But the good news of the Christian religion is that although we can do nothing, God has done something. He has done what needs to be done. He has communicated with us. In other words, in addition to the general but limited revelation of himself in nature, God has provided a special revelation designed to lead those who did not know God and did not want to know God to a saving knowledge of him. This special revelation has three stages. First, there is *redemption in history*. This centers in the work of the Lord Jesus Christ. He died in the place of sinners and rose as proof of their divine justification. Second, there is a *revelation in writing*. This is the Bible. God has provided interpretive records of what he has done for our redemption. Finally, there is the *application* of these truths to the mind and heart of the individual by the Holy Spirit. As a result the individual is born again, receives the Lord Jesus Christ as his Savior, and is enabled to follow him faithfully until life's end.

It is evident, however, that in this three-stage special revelation the Bible is of critical importance. In the Bible alone we learn of God's redemption of sinners in Christ; through the Bible the Spirit speaks to individuals. Therefore, as Calvin says, "Our wisdom ought to be nothing else than to embrace with humble teachableness, and at least without finding fault, whatever is taught in Sacred Scripture."[1]

Without the Scriptures our imagined wisdom runs to foolishness. With the Scriptures and under the guidance of the Holy Spirit we are able to learn who God is, what he has done for us, and how we can respond to him and live our lives in fellowship with him.

God Has Spoken

The importance of the Bible lies in its being the Word of God written. And the first reason for believing the Bible to be this is the Bible's own teaching about itself. That is where all people and particularly Christians should start. Many appeal to the Scriptures in defense of basic doctrines: the doctrine of God, the deity of Christ, the atonement, the resurrection, the nature of the church, the work of the Holy Spirit, the final judgment and many other points of theology. They do so rightly. But if the Bible is authoritative and accurate in these

matters, there is no reason why it should not be authoritative
and accurate when speaking about itself.

When we take this approach, the first verse to look at is 2
Timothy 3:16. Here the New Testament speaks of the Old
Testament, noting that "all scripture is inspired by God." The
English phrase "is inspired by" (RSV) or "is given by inspiration of" (KJV) translates only one Greek word. This word, as
B. B. Warfield pointed out at the beginning of this century,
"very distinctly does not mean 'inspired of God.' "[2] That English phrase has come down to us from the Latin Vulgate (_divin-
itus inspirata_) through the translation of Wycliffe ("Al Scripture of God ynspyrid is . . .") and other early English versions.
But the Greek word does not mean "inspired." It literally
means "God-breathed." This word has never been correctly
translated by any English version until publication in 1973 of
the New International Bible: New Testament.

The Greek word _theopneustos_ combines the word for "God"
(_theos_) and the word for "breath" or "spirit" (_pneustos_).
In English we have the word for God preserved in the words
theology, theophany, monotheism, atheist, and in the names _Dor-
othy, Theodore_ and others. _Pneuma_ is preserved in the words
pneumatic and _pneumonia._ Together the words teach that the
Scriptures are the direct result of the breathing out of God.
Warfield writes,

> _The Greek term has . . . nothing to say of inspiring or of inspira-
> tion: it speaks only of a "spiring" or "spiration." What it says of
> Scripture is, not that it is "breathed into by God" or that it is the
> product of the Divine "inbreathing" into its human authors, but
> that it is breathed out by God. . . . When Paul declares, then, that
> "every scripture," or "all scripture" is the product of the Divine
> breath, "is God-breathed," he asserts with as much energy as he
> could employ that Scripture is the product of a specifically Divine
> operation._ [3]

Some things recorded in the Bible, of course, are merely the
words of weak and erring men. But when that is the case, the

words are identified as such. To give one extreme example, in the early chapters of the book of Job we read, "Skin for skin! All that a man has he will give for his life" (Job 2:4). But that is not true, at least not in all cases. How is this to be explained? When we read the chapter carefully we see that the words were spoken by the devil, who is elsewhere described as the father of all falsehood (Jn. 8:44). Similarly, in the rest of the book we find long chapters filled with the vain and sometimes faulty advice of Job's comforters. But their words are not fully true, and suddenly God breaks into the nonsense to ask, "Who is this that darkens counsel by words without knowledge?" (Job 38:2). Here God specifically denies that the words of Job's counselors are true. The truth is that they spoke the words they are reported as having spoken.

In the light of such examples we see that the Bible carries absolute authority as to the factualness of the narratives, but not necessarily as to the views expressed by the sinful men and women (or the devil) who appear in its pages. On the other hand, whenever God speaks either directly or through one of his prophets there is not only perfect accuracy but absolute authority as well. It has been noted that in the Pentateuch alone the words "the LORD said" occur almost eight hundred times and that the words "Thus saith the LORD" are a recurring refrain throughout the prophets. In these passages we deal with the very words, works and sentiments of God.

"It Says"/"God Says"

Next to the verse from 2 Timothy may be placed a double series of passages, collected by Warfield, showing clearly that the New Testament writers identified the Bible which they possessed, the Old Testament, with the living voice of God. "In one of these classes of passages," writes Warfield, "the Scriptures are spoken of as if they were God; in the other, God is spoken of as if he were the Scriptures: in the two together, God and the Scriptures are brought into such conjunction as to show that in point of directness of authority no distinction was made between them."[4] The sensitive reader of the Bible can only conclude that the unique and divine character of the sacred books was by no means an invented or abstract affirmation of the biblical writers, but rather a basic assumption behind all that they taught or wrote.

Examples of the first class of passages are such as these: Galatians 3:8, "The scripture, foreseeing that God would justify the heathen through faith, preached before the gospel unto Abraham, saying, In thee shall all the nations be blessed" (Gen. 12:1-3); Romans 9:17, "The scripture saith unto Pharaoh, Even for this same purpose have I raised thee up" (Ex. 9:16). It was not, however, the Scripture (which did not exist at the time) that, foreseeing God's purposes of grace in the future, spoke these precious words to Abraham, but God himself in his own person: it was not the not yet existent Scripture that made this announcement to Pharaoh, but God himself through the mouth of his prophet Moses. These acts could be attributed to "Scripture" only as the result of such a habitual identification, in the mind of the writer, of the text of Scripture with God as speaking, that it became natural to use the term "Scripture says," when what was really intended was "God, as recorded in Scripture, said."

Examples of the other class of passages are such as these: Matthew 19:4, 5, "And he answered and said, Have ye not read, that he which made them at the beginning made them male and female, and said, For this cause shall a man leave his father and mother, and shall cleave to his wife, and the twain shall be one flesh?" (Gen. 2:24); Hebrews 3:7, "Wherefore as the Holy Ghost saith, Today if ye will hear his voice," etc. (Ps. 95:7); Acts 4:24, 25, "Thou art God ... who by the mouth of thy servant David hast said, Why did the heathen rage, and the people imagine vain things" (Ps. 2:1); Acts 13:34, 35, "He that raised him up from the dead, now no more to return to corruption, ... hath spoken in this wise, I will give you the holy and sure blessings of David" (Is. 55:3);

"because he saith also in another [Psalm], Thou wilt not give thy holy one to see corruption" (Ps. 16:10); Hebrews 1:6, "And when he again bringeth in the first born into the world, he saith, And let all the angels of God worship him" (Deut. 32:43); "and of angels he saith, Who maketh his angels wings, and his ministers a flame of fire" (Ps. 104:4); "but of the Son, He saith, Thy throne, O God, is for ever and ever," etc. (Ps. 45:6) and "Thou, LORD, in the beginning," etc. (Ps. 102:25). It is not God, however, in whose mouth these sayings are placed in the text of the Old Testament: they are the words of others, recorded in the text of Scripture as spoken to or of God. They could be attributed to God only through such habitual identification, in the minds of the writers, of the text of Scripture with the utterances of God that it had become natural to use the term "God says" when what was really intended was "Scripture, the Word of God, says."

The two sets of passages, together, thus show an absolute identification, in the minds of these writers, of "Scripture" with the speaking of God.[5]

It is not that Scripture "contains" the Word of God or "witnesses" to the Word of God. It is that Scripture *is* the Word of God, spoken by God and preserved at his direction by the biblical writers.

Moved by God

None of the preceding discussion is meant to deny the genuine human element in Scripture. In 2 Peter 1:21, Peter writes, "No prophecy ever came by the impulse of man, but men moved by the Holy Spirit spoke from God." It can hardly be overemphasized in the light of some current misunderstandings that Peter does acknowledge that people had a part in writing Scripture. He says, "men . . . spoke."

The biblical writers wrote out of their own experience. They used their own vocabulary. The literary polish of their writings varies. They sometimes use secular sources. They are selective. In many ways the books of the Bible bear evidence of having been written by people who were very human and very much people of their time.

Yet the books of the Old and New Testaments bear evidence of being something more. Peter says that these writers "spoke from God." He tells us that the biblical writers were "moved by the Holy Spirit." The word translated "moved" is significant. It is used by Luke to describe the coming of the Holy Spirit at Pentecost as the "*rush* of a mighty wind" (Acts 2:2). Again, Luke employs the word in the dramatic account of the Mediterranean storm that ultimately destroyed the ship taking Paul to Rome. Luke notes that the ship was *carried along* by the wind. "When the ship was caught and could not face the wind, we gave way to it and were *driven*" (Acts 27:15); "they lowered the gear, and so were *driven*" (v. 17). Luke was saying that the ship was at the mercy of the storm. It did not cease to be a ship, but it did cease to have control over its course and destination.

Similarly, Peter teaches that the writers of the Bible were borne along in their writing to produce the words which God intended to be recorded. They wrote as people but as people moved by the Holy Spirit. The result was the revelation of God.

The verse in 2 Peter does not imply anything about a particular method by which the biblical writers became aware of God's Word and transcribed it. The methods that God used to communicate his revelation to the biblical writers varied. Some apparently wrote as people might write today, collecting material and composing it to bring out the most significant events or emphases. Such were John, the author of the fourth Gospel, and Luke, the author of the third Gospel and of Acts (Jn. 20:30; Lk. 1:1-4; Acts 1:1-2). They did not receive their books from God by dictation. Moses received a revelation of the law on Mt. Sinai in the midst of fire, smoke and thunder (Ex. 19:18-19). The Lord came to Daniel in a vision (Dan. 2:19), as he did perhaps also to the apostle Paul on one occasion (Gal. 1:11-12). Isaiah claimed to have heard the voice of the Lord as he would have heard the voice of another human being. "The LORD of hosts has revealed himself in my ears" (Is. 22:14). The methods are clearly varied, but the result is the same. The product is the specific revelation of God.

Most of the texts mentioned thus far have had to do with the Old Testament. But there are also texts which indicate that the teaching of the New Testament about the Old Testament applies to the New Testament writings too. Thus, Paul writes of the gospel which he had preached: "We also thank God constantly for this, that when you received the word of God which you heard from us, you accepted it not as the word of men but as what it really is, the word of God, which is at work in you believers" (1 Thess. 2:13, compare Gal. 1:11-12). Similarly, Peter places the Pauline letters in the same category as the Old Testament. "Our beloved brother Paul wrote to you according to the wisdom given him, speaking of this as he does in all his letters. There are some things in them hard to understand, which the ignorant and unstable twist to their own destruction, as they do *the other scriptures*" (2 Pet. 3:15-16).

Of course, the New Testament does not speak of itself with the same frequency and in exactly the same manner as it speaks of the Old Testament since the New Testament books had not been collected into an authoritative volume during the lifetime of the writers. Nevertheless, on several occasions the New Testament writers do speak of their writings as the words of God. In some cases, when a New Testament book was written late enough to know of other New Testament writings, the later book speaks of the earlier ones in the same terms that Christians and Jews used for the Old Testament.

The Witness of Jesus Christ
The most important reason for believing the Bible to be the Word of God written and hence the sole authority for Chris-

tians in all matters of faith and conduct is the teaching of Jesus Christ. Today it is common for some to contrast the Bible's authority unfavorably with Christ's. But such a contrast is unjustifiable. Jesus so identified himself with Scripture and so interpreted his ministry in the light of Scripture that it is impossible to weaken the authority of one without at the same time weakening the authority of the other.

Christ's high regard for the Old Testament is first seen by the fact that he appealed to it as an infallible authority. When tempted by the devil in the wilderness, Jesus replied three times by quotations from Deuteronomy (Mt. 4:1-11). He replied to the question of the Sadducees about the heavenly status of marriage and the reality of the resurrection (Lk. 20:27-40), first by a rebuke that they did not know either the Scriptures or the power of God and second, by a direct quotation from Exodus 3:6, "I am the God of your father, the God of Abraham, the God of Isaac, and the God of Jacob." On many occasions Jesus appealed to Scripture in support of his actions, as in defense of his cleansing of the temple (Mk. 11: 15-17) or in reference to his submission to the cross (Mt. 26:53-54). He taught that the "scripture cannot be broken" (Jn. 10:35). He declared, "Till heaven and earth pass away, not an iota, not a dot, will pass from the law until all is accomplished" (Mt. 5:18).

Matthew 5:18 deserves some additional consideration. It is evident, even as we read the phrase after a space of some two thousand years, that the words "not an iota, not a dot" were a common expression referring to the most minute parts of the Mosaic law. The iota was the smallest letter of the Hebrew alphabet, the letter that we would transliterate by an *i* or *y*. In written Hebrew it resembled a comma, though it was written near the top of the letters rather than near the bottom. The dot (or tittle, KJV) was what we would call a serif, the tiny projection on letters that distinguishes a roman typeface from a more modern one. In many Bibles Psalm 119 is divided into twenty-two sections each beginning with a different letter of the Hebrew alphabet. If one's Bible is well printed, the English reader can see what a dot is by comparing the Hebrew letter before verse 9 with the Hebrew letter before verse 81. The first letter is a *beth*. The second is a *kaph*. The only difference between them is the serif. The same feature distinguishes *daleth* from *resh* and *vau* from *zayin*. According to Jesus, then, not even an "i" or a "serif" of the law would be lost until the whole law was fulfilled.

But what can give the law so permanent a character? Obviously nothing human, for all things human pass away. The only basis for the law's imperishable quality is that it is actually divine. The reason it will not pass away is that it is the Word of the true, living and eternal God. That is the substance of Christ's teaching.

Second, Jesus saw his life as a fulfillment of Scripture. He consciously submitted himself to it. He began his ministry with a quotation from Isaiah 61:1-2. "The Spirit of the Lord is upon me, because he has anointed me to preach good news to the poor. He has sent me to proclaim release to the captives and recovering of sight to the blind, to set at liberty those who are oppressed, to proclaim the acceptable year of the Lord" (Lk. 4:18-19). When he had finished reading he put the scroll down and said, "Today this scripture has been fulfilled in your hearing" (v. 21). Jesus was claiming to be the Messiah, the one about whom Isaiah had written. He was identifying his forthcoming ministry with the lines set out for it in Scripture.

Later in his ministry we find disciples of John the Baptist coming to Jesus with John's question, "Are you he who is to come, or shall we look for another?" (Mt. 11:3). Jesus answered by a second reference to this section of Isaiah's prophecy. He said, in effect, "Don't take my word for who I am. Look at what Isaiah foretold about the Messiah. Then see if I'm fulfilling it." Jesus challenged people to evaluate his ministry in the light of God's Word.

The Gospel of John shows Jesus talking to the Jewish rulers about authority, and the climax of what he says has to do entirely with Scripture. He says that nobody would ever believe in him who had not first believed in the writings of Moses, for Moses wrote about him. "You search the scriptures, because you think that in them you have eternal life; and it is they that bear witness to me. . . . Do not think that I shall accuse you to the Father; it is Moses who accuses you, on whom you set your hope. If you believed Moses, you would believe me, for he wrote of me. But if you do not believe his writings, how will you believe my words?" (Jn. 5:39, 45-47).

At the end of Jesus' life, as he is hanging on the cross, he is again thinking of Scripture. He says, "My God, my God, why hast thou forsaken me?" (a quotation from Ps. 22:1). He says that he thirsts. They give him a sponge filled with vinegar that Psalm 69:21 might be fulfilled. Three days later, after the resurrection, he is on the way to Emmaus with two of his disciples, chiding them because they have not used Scripture to understand the necessity of his suffering. He says, "O foolish men, and slow of heart to believe all that the prophets have spoken! Was it not necessary that the Christ should suffer these things and enter into his glory?" Then, "beginning with Moses and all the prophets, he interpreted to them in all the scriptures the things concerning himself" (Lk. 24:25-27).

On the basis of these and many other passages it is beyond doubt that Jesus highly esteemed the Old Testament and constantly submitted to it as to an authoritative revelation. He taught that the Scriptures bore a witness to him, just as he bore a witness to them. Because they are the words of God, Jesus assumed their complete reliability, in whole and to the smallest part.

Jesus also endorsed the New Testament though in a different form from his endorsement of the Old Testament (because, of course, the New Testament had not yet been written). He foresaw the writing of the New Testament. So he chose and authorized the apostles to be the recipients of the new revelation.

There were two qualifications of an apostle, as Acts 1:21-26 and other passages indicate. First, the apostle was to be one who had known Jesus during the days of his earthly ministry and had been a witness of his resurrection in particular (vv. 21-22). Paul's apostleship was undoubtedly challenged at this point because he became a Christian after the return of Christ to heaven and thus hadn't known him in the flesh. But Paul cited his vision of the resurrected Christ on the road to Damascus as having met this requirement. "Am I not an apostle? . . . Have I not seen Jesus our Lord?" (1 Cor. 9:1).

The second requirement was that Jesus had chosen the apostle for his unique role and task. As part of this he promised a unique giving of the Holy Spirit so that they would remember, understand and be able to record the truths concerning his ministry. "But the Counselor, the Holy Spirit, whom the Father will send in my name, he will teach you all things, and bring to your remembrance all that I have said to you" (Jn. 14:26). Similarly, "I have yet many things to say to you, but you cannot bear them now. When the Spirit of truth comes, he will guide you into all the truth; for he will not speak on his own authority, but whatever he hears he will speak, and he will declare to you the things that are to come. He will glorify me, for he will take what is mine and declare it to you" (Jn. 16:12-14).

Did the apostles fulfill their commission? Yes, they did. The New Testament is the result. What is more, the early church recognized their role. For when it came time to declare officially what books were to be included in the canon of the New Testament the decisive factor was perceived to be whether or not they were written by the apostles or bore apostolic endorsement. The church did not create the canon which, if it had, would place itself over Scripture. Rather the church submitted to Scripture as a higher authority.

The Question

We end this chapter with an obvious question. Do we believe these teachings? Do we believe that the Bible is indeed the written Word of God in accord with its own teaching and that of the Lord Jesus Christ?

It is popular today to doubt this teaching. This has caused much current confusion in theology and in the Christian church. But the doubt is not new. It is the most fundamental and original of all doubts. It is found on the lips of Satan in the earliest chapters of the Bible. "He [the serpent] said to the woman, 'Did God say, "You shall not eat of any tree of the garden"?' " (Gen. 3:1). The question is: Can God be trusted? Is the Bible truly his Word? Do we believe this without any mental reservations? If we do question the Word of God and if we have mental reservations about its authority, we will never be interested in true Bible study nor will we come into the fullness of wisdom about God and ourselves that he desires for us. On the other hand, if we do accept these truths, we will want to study the Bible, and we will grow in knowledge and devotion. In fact, the study of Scripture will bless us. The text that began this chapter goes on to say, "All scripture is inspired by God [is God-breathed] and profitable for teaching, for reproof, for correction, and for training in righteousness, that the man of God may be complete, equipped for every good work" (2 Tim. 3:16-17).

4 THE AUTHORITY OF THE SCRIPTURES

A primary cause of the confusion within the Christian church today is its lack of a valid authority. There have been attempts to supply this authority through the pronouncements of church councils, existential encounter with an intangible "word" of God and other means. But none of these recent approaches can claim to be very successful. What is wrong? What is the source of the Christian's authority?

The classical Protestant answer is the revealed Word of God, the Bible. The Bible is authoritative because it is not the words of mere humans, though humans were the channels by which it came to us, but it is the direct result of the "breathing-out" of God. It is his product. But there is another level on which the question of authority may be raised. This relates to the way in which we become convinced of the Bible's authority. What is there about the Bible or the study of the Bible that should convince us that it is indeed God's Word?

The human aspect of the authority question takes us a bit further into what we mean when we say that the Bible is the

Word of God, for the full meaning of that statement is not only that God has spoken to give us the Bible but also that he continues to speak through it to individuals. In other words, as individuals study the Bible, God speaks to them in their study and transforms them by the truths they find there. There is a direct encounter of the individual believer with God. It is what Luther meant when he declared at the Diet of Worms, "My conscience has been taken captive by the Word of God." It is what Calvin meant when he declared that "Scripture indeed is self-authenticated."[1]

Nothing but direct experience will ever ultimately convince anybody that the Bible's words are the authentic and authoritative words of God. As Calvin said, "The same spirit, therefore, who has spoken through the mouths of the prophets must penetrate into our hearts to persuade us that they faithfully proclaimed what has been divinely commanded."[2]

The Bible is something more than a body of revealed truths, a collection of books verbally inspired of God. It is also the living voice of God. The living God speaks through its pages. Therefore, it is not to be valued as a sacred object to be placed on a shelf and neglected, but as holy ground, where people's hearts and minds may come into vital contact with the living, gracious and disturbing God. For a proper perspective on Scripture and for a valid understanding of revelation there must be a constant interworking of these factors: an infallible and authoritative Word, the activity of the Holy Spirit in interpreting and applying that Word and a receptive human heart. No true knowledge of God takes place without these elements.

Reformation Insight

The assurance that God had spoken to them directly through his holy Scriptures gave the Reformers their unique boldness. The formation of that truth theologically was the fundamentally new element in the Reformation.

The Reformation battle cry was *Sola Scriptura,* "Scripture

alone." But *Sola Scriptura* meant more to the Reformers than that God has revealed himself in the propositions of the Bible. The new element was not that the Bible, being given by God, speaks with God's own authority. The Roman Church held to that as well as the Reformers. The new element, as Packer points out,

> *was the belief, borne in upon the Reformers by their own experience of Bible study, that Scripture can and does interpret itself to the faithful from within–Scripture is its own interpreter,* Scriptura sui ipsius interpres, *as Luther puts it–so that not only does it not need Popes or Councils to tell us, as from God, what it means; it can actually challenge Papal and conciliar pronouncements, convince them of being ungodly and untrue, and require the faithful to part company with them. . . . As Scripture was the only* source *from which sinners might gain true knowledge of God and godliness, so Scripture was the only* judge *of what the church had in each age ventured to say in her Lord's name.* [3]

In Luther's time the Roman Church had weakened the authority of the Bible by exalting human traditions to the stature of Scripture and by insisting that the teaching of the Bible could be communicated to Christian people only through the mediation of popes, councils and priests. The Reformers restored biblical authority by holding that the living God speaks to his people directly and authoritatively through its pages.

The Reformers called the activity of God by which the truth of his Word is borne in upon the mind and consciences of his people, "the internal witness of the Holy Spirit." They stressed that such activity was the subjective or internal counterpart of the objective or external revelation, and often referred to texts from John's writings. "The wind blows where it wills, and you hear the sound of it, but you do not know whence it comes or whither it goes; so it is with every one who is born of the Spirit" (Jn. 3:8). "But you have been anointed by the Holy One, and you all know. . . . But the anointing which you received from him abides in you, and you have no need that any one should teach you; as his anointing teaches you about everything, and is true, and is no lie, just as it has taught you, abide in him" (1 Jn. 2:20, 27). "And the Spirit is the witness, because the Spirit is the truth" (1 Jn. 5:7).

The same idea is present in Paul's writings.

We have received not the spirit of the world, but the Spirit which is from God, that we might understand the gifts bestowed on us by God. And we impart this in words not taught by human wisdom but taught by the Spirit, interpreting spiritual truths to those who possess the Spirit. The unspiritual man does not receive the gifts of the Spirit of God, for they are folly to him, and he is not able to understand them because they are spiritually discerned. The spiritual man judges all things, but is himself to be judged by no one. (1 Cor. 2:12-15)

I do not cease to give thanks for you, remembering you in my prayers, that the God of our Lord Jesus Christ, the Father of glory, may give you a spirit of wisdom and of revelation in the knowledge of him, having the eyes of your hearts enlightened, that you may know what is the hope to which he has called you, what are the riches of his glorious inheritance in the saints, and what is the immeasurable greatness of his power in us who believe, according to the working of his great might which he accomplished in Christ when he raised him from the dead and made him sit at his right hand in the heavenly places. (Eph. 1:16-20)

Taken together these texts teach that not only our rebirth but our entire growth in spiritual wisdom and the knowledge of God is the result of the working of the divine Spirit upon our life and mind through the Scriptures, and that no spiritual understanding is possible apart from this activity. The witness of the Holy Spirit is, therefore, the effectual reason why the Bible is received as the final authority in all matters of faith and practice by those who are God's children.

The Book That Understands Me

When we begin to read the Bible and are spoken to by the

Holy Spirit as we read it, several things happen. First, the reading affects us as no other reading does.

Dr. Emile Cailliet was a French philosopher who eventually settled in America and became a professor at Princeton Theological Seminary in New Jersey. He had been brought up with a naturalistic education. He had never shown the slightest interest in spiritual things. He had never seen a Bible. But World War 1 came, and as he sat in the trenches he found himself reflecting on the inadequacy of his world and life view. He asked himself the same questions Levin had asked in Leo Tolstoy's _Anna Karenina,_ while sitting beside the bed of his dying brother: Where did life come from? What did it all mean, if anything? What value are scientific laws or theories in the face of reality? Cailliet later wrote, "Like Levin, I too felt, not with my reason but with my whole being, that I was destined to perish miserably when the hour came."

During the long night watches Cailliet began to long for what he came to call "a book that would understand me." He was highly educated, but he knew of no such book. Thus, when he was later wounded and released from the army and returned to his studies, he determined that he would prepare such a book secretly for his own use. As he read for his courses, he would file away passages that seemed to speak to his condition. Afterward he would copy them over in a leather-bound book. He hoped that the quotations, which he carefully indexed and numbered, would lead him from fear and anguish to release and jubilation.

At last the day came when he had put the finishing touches to his book, "the book that would understand me." He went out and sat down under a tree and opened the anthology. He began to read, but instead of release and jubilation, a growing disappointment began to come over him as he recognized that instead of speaking to his condition, the various passages only reminded him of their context and of his own work in searching them out and recording them. Then he knew that the whole undertaking simply would not work, for the book was a book of his own making. It carried no strength of persuasion. Dejected, he returned it to his pocket.

At that very moment his wife (who knew nothing of the project) came by with an interesting story. She had been walking in their tiny French village that afternoon and had stumbled upon a small Huguenot chapel. She had never seen it before, but she had gone in and had asked for a Bible, much to her own surprise. The elderly pastor had given her one. She began apologizing to her husband, for she knew his feelings about the Christian faith. But he wasn't listening to her apology. "A Bible, you say? Where is it? Show me," he said. "I have never seen one before." When she produced it he rushed to his study and began to read. In his own words,

> *I opened it and "chanced" upon the Beatitudes! I read, and read, and read—now aloud with an indescribable warmth surging within. . . . I could not find words to express my awe and wonder. And suddenly the realization dawned upon me: This* was *the Book that would understand me! I needed it so much, yet, unaware, I had attempted to write my own—in vain. I continued to read deeply into the night, mostly from the gospels. And lo and behold, as I looked through them, the One of whom they spoke, the One who spoke and acted in them, became alive to me. This vivid experience marked the beginning of my understanding of prayer. It also proved to be my initiation to the notion of Presence which later would prove so crucial in my theological thinking.*
>
> *The providential circumstances amid which the Book had found me now made it clear that while it seemed absurd to speak of a book understanding a man, this could be said of the Bible because its pages were animated by the Presence of the Living God and the Power of His mighty acts. To this God I prayed that night, and the God who answered* was *the same God of whom it was spoken in the Book.* [4]

In all ages God's people have discovered the Reformation insight. Here is Calvin's expression of the same truth:

*Now this power which is peculiar to Scripture is clear from the fact
that of human writings, however artfully polished, there is none
capable of affecting us at all comparably. Read Demosthenes or
Cicero; read Plato, Aristotle, and others of that tribe. They will,
I admit, allure you, delight you, move you, enrapture you in wonderful measure. But betake yourself from them to this sacred reading. Then, in spite of yourself, so deeply will it affect you, so
penetrate your heart, so fix itself in your very marrow, that compared with its deep impression, such vigor as the orators and
philosophers have will nearly vanish. Consequently, it is easy to see
that the Sacred Scriptures, which so far surpass all gifts and graces
of human endeavor, breathe something divine.* [5]

Another example is recorded toward the end of Luke's Gospel. Jesus had just risen from the dead and had begun to appear to the disciples. Two of these, Cleopas and possibly his
wife, were returning to their home town of Emmaus when
Jesus drew close to them on the road. They did not recognize him. When he asked why they were downcast they replied by telling him what had happened in Jerusalem at the
time of the Passover. They told him about Jesus, "who was a
prophet mighty in deed and word before God and all the
people." They told him how the chief priests and rulers "delivered him up to be condemned to death, and crucified him."
They had been in Jerusalem that very morning and had heard
tales from the women who had been to the tomb, reporting
that the body was gone and that angels had appeared proclaiming that Jesus had been made alive. But they didn't
believe in resurrections. They hadn't even bothered to go to
the tomb to see for themselves, although they were within a
short walk of it. The dream was over. Jesus was dead. They
were going home.

But Jesus began to talk to them and explain the mission of
the Christ, teaching them from the Scriptures. He said, "O
foolish men, and slow of heart to believe all that the prophets
have spoken! Was it not necessary that the Christ should suf-

fer these things and enter into his glory?" Then beginning
with Moses and going through all the prophets, he explained
to them out of the Scriptures the things they said about himself.

At last they came to where the two disciples lived. They in-
vited Jesus in, and he revealed himself to them as they ate together. He vanished, and they at once returned to Jerusalem
to tell the other disciples what had happened. Their own
testimony was this: "Did not our hearts burn within us while
he talked to us on the road, while he opened to us the scriptures?" (Lk. 24:13-32). They were convicted by the Word of
God. In this instance Jesus himself fulfilled the role of the
Holy Spirit by interpreting the Bible to his disciples and by
applying its truths to them.

The Bible also changes us. We become different men and
women as a result of encountering it. A section of the thir-
teenth chapter of Romans changed the life of St. Augustine as
he turned to the Bible in the garden of a friend's estate near
Milan, Italy. Luther tells how in meditating upon the Scriptures while secluded in the Wartburg Castle, he felt himself to
be "reborn," and tells how Romans 1:17 became for him "a
gate to heaven." John Wesley's meditation upon Scripture led
to his conversion in the little meeting in Aldersgate. J. B.
Phillips writes,

> *Some years before the publication of the New English Bible, I was*
> *invited by the BBC to discuss the problems of translation with Dr.*
> *E. V. Rieu, who had himself recently produced a translation of the*
> *four Gospels for Penguin Classics. Towards the end of the discus-*
> *sion Dr. Rieu was asked about his general approach to the task,*
> *and his reply was this:*
>
> *"My personal reason for doing this was my own intense desire*
> *to satisfy myself as to the authenticity and the spiritual content of*
> *the Gospels. And, if I received any new light by an intensive study*
> *of the Greek originals, to pass it on to others. I approached them*
> *in the same spirit as I would have approached them had they been*

presented to me as recently discovered Greek manuscripts."

_A few minutes later I asked him, "Did you get the feeling that
the whole material is extraordinarily alive? . . . I got the feeling
that the whole thing was alive even while one was translating.
Even though one did a dozen versions of a particular passage, it
was still living. Did you get that feeling?"_

_Dr. Rieu replied, "I got the deepest feeling that I possibly could
have experienced. It–changed me; my work changed me. And I
came to the conclusion that these words bear the seal of–the Son
of man and God. And they're the Magna Carta of the human
spirit."_

Phillips concludes, "I found it particularly thrilling to hear a
man who is a scholar of the first rank as well as a man of wisdom and experience openly admitting that these words written long ago were alive with power. They bore to him, as to
me, the ring of truth."[6]

One Subject

Another result of reading the Bible is that the Holy Spirit who
speaks in its pages will direct the student to Jesus. The Bible
contains many varieties of material. It covers hundreds of
years of history. Still, the object of the Bible in each of its
parts is to point to Jesus, and this goal is carried out on the
subjective level by Christ's Spirit. Jesus said, "But when the
Counselor comes, whom I shall send to you from the Father,
even the Spirit of truth, who proceeds from the Father, he will
bear witness to me" (Jn. 15:26). Since the role of the Holy
Spirit is to point to Jesus in the Scriptures, we can be sure that
we are listening to the voice of the Holy Spirit when that
happens.

"Isn't the Bible mostly history?" a person might ask. "How
can Jesus be its subject in the Old Testament? And how can
the Holy Spirit point us to him?" Jesus becomes the subject of
the Old Testament in two ways: (1) by fitting in with its general
themes and (2) by fulfilling specific prophecies found there.

One main theme of the Old Testament is *human sin* and our resultant need. The Bible begins with the story of the creation. But no sooner is this story told (in the first chapter of Genesis) than we are also told of the Fall of the human race. Instead of being humbly and gratefully dependent upon our Creator, as we should have been, we were soon in a state of rebellion against God. We went our own way instead of God's. So the consequences of sin (ultimately, death) came upon the human race.

In the rest of the Old Testament we see these consequences unfolding: the murder of Abel, the corruption leading up to the flood, demonism, sexual perversions, eventually even tragedy for the chosen nation of Israel in spite of great blessings. The Old Testament is best summarized in David's psalm of repentance, which ought properly to be the psalm of the whole human race. "Have mercy on me, O God, according to thy steadfast love; according to thy abundant mercy blot out my transgressions. Wash me thoroughly from my iniquity, and cleanse me from my sin! For I know my transgressions, and my sin is ever before me. . . . Behold, I was brought forth in iniquity, and in sin did my mother conceive me" (Ps. 51: 1-3, 5).

Here is one important biblical doctrine. But if we understand it right, even this doctrine is not an end in itself. The truth of our sin and need is expounded in the Bible because the Bible is also able to point to Christ as the solution to the dilemma.

A second Old Testament theme is the existence of a *God who acts in love* to redeem sinners. God the Father did this throughout the Old Testament period. At the same time, as he did it, he pointed to the coming of his Son who would redeem men and women perfectly and forever.

When Adam and Eve sinned, sin separated them from the Creator. They tried to hide. God, however, came to them in the cool of the evening, calling them. It is true that God spoke in judgment, as he had to do. He revealed the consequences of their sin. Still, he also killed animals, clothed the man and woman with skins, covering their shame, and began his teaching of the way of salvation through sacrifice. In the same story he spoke to Satan revealing the coming of One who would one day defeat him forever: "He shall bruise your head, and you shall bruise his heel" (Gen. 3:15).

Nine chapters later we find another, somewhat veiled reference to the "seed" who shall crush Satan. It is God's first great promise to Abraham, stressing that in him all nations would be blessed (Gen. 12:3; 22:18). The blessing referred to is certainly not a blessing to come to all people through Abraham personally. It is not a blessing to come through all Jews indiscriminately, for all Jews are not even theists. The foretold blessing was to come through the seed of Abraham, the promised seed, the Messiah. Thus, years later the apostle Paul, who knew this text, used it to show: (1) that the seed was the Lord Jesus, (2) that the promise to Abraham was one of blessing through him and (3) that the blessing was to come through Christ's work of redemption (Gal. 3:13-16).

An interesting prophecy was spoken by the Lord through Balaam, a shifty, half-hearted prophet of Moses' day. Balak, a king who was hostile to Israel, had hired Balaam to curse the Jewish people. But every time Balaam opened his mouth, blessings on the people came out instead. On one occasion he said, "A star shall come forth out of Jacob, and a scepter shall rise out of Israel. . . . By Jacob shall dominion be exercised" (Num. 24:17, 19).

As he was dying, the patriarch Jacob said, "The scepter shall not depart from Judah, nor the ruler's staff from between his feet, until he comes to whom it belongs; and to him shall be the obedience of the peoples" (Gen. 49:10).

Moses also spoke of the One who would come: "The LORD your God will raise up for you a prophet like me from among you, from your brethren—him you shall heed" (Deut. 18:15).

And again, with God speaking, "I will put my words in his mouth, and he shall speak to them all that I command him" (v. 18b).

The book of Psalms contains great prophecies. The second psalm tells of Christ's victory and rule over the nations of this earth. This psalm was a popular one with the early Christians (see Acts 4). Psalm 16 foretells the resurrection (v. 10; see Acts 2:31). In Psalms 22, 23 and 24 we have three portraits of the Lord Jesus: the suffering Savior, the compassionate Shepherd and the King. Other psalms speak of other aspects of his life and ministry. Psalm 110 returns to the theme of his rule, looking for the day when Jesus shall take his seat at the right hand of the Father when all his enemies shall be made his "footstool."

Details of Christ's life, death and resurrection occur in the books of the prophets—in Isaiah, Daniel, Jeremiah, Ezekiel, Hosea, Zechariah and others.

The Lord Jesus Christ and his work are the chief subjects of the Bible. It is the work of the Holy Spirit to reveal him. As the revelation takes place the Bible becomes understandable, Scripture bears witness to Scripture, and the authority and power of the living God are sensed to be surging through its pages.

Word and Spirit

The combination of an objective, written revelation and its subjective interpretation to the individual by God's Spirit is the key to the Christian doctrine of the knowledge of God. This combination keeps us from two serious errors.

The first is the error of overspiritualizing revelation. This is the error that entangled the Anabaptist "enthusiasts" in Calvin's day and which has since entrapped many of their followers. The enthusiasts laid claim to private, Spirit-given revelations as justification for their decisions and conduct. But these were often contrary to the express teaching of the Word of God, as, for example, their occasional decision to stop working and gather for the anticipated return of the Lord. Without the objective Word there was no way to judge such "revelations" or to keep the individuals from error who were caught up in them. Calvin wrote in reference to this dilemma:

> The Holy Spirit so inheres in his truth, which he expresses in Scripture, that only when its proper reverence and dignity are given to the Word does the Holy Spirit show forth his power.... The children of God ... see themselves, without the Spirit of God, bereft of the whole light of truth, so are not unaware that the Word is the instrument by which the Lord dispenses the illumination of his Spirit to believers. For they know no other Spirit than him who dwelt and spoke in the apostles, and by whose oracles they are continually recalled to the hearing of the Word.[7]

On the other hand, the combination of an objective Word and a subjective application of that Word by God's Spirit also keeps us from the error of overintellectualizing God's truth. That error was evident in the diligent Bible study habits of the scribes and Pharisees in Jesus' time. The scribes and Pharisees were not slothful students. They were meticulous in their pursuit of Bible knowledge, even to the point of counting the individual letters of the Bible books. Yet Jesus rebuked them saying, "You search the scriptures, because you think that in them you have eternal life; and it is they that bear witness to me" (Jn. 5:39).

To know God we must be taught from the Bible by the Holy Spirit. It is only then that a full awareness of the nature of the Bible and its authority is borne home upon our minds and hearts, and we find ourselves taking a firm stand upon that cherished revelation.

5   THE PROOF OF THE SCRIPTURES

The chief evidence for the Bible's being the Word of God is the internal testimony of the Holy Spirit to that truth. Without such testimony the truthfulness of Scripture will never impress itself adequately upon a reader. But that doesn't mean that there are no rational supports for one's conviction. The rational arguments should be known by the mature Christian as well as by anyone who is just beginning to consider the claims of Christianity.

What are these arguments? Some have already been suggested. First, there are the claims of the Scriptures themselves. The books of the Bible claim to be the Word of God, and, while this in itself does not prove that they are, nevertheless it is a fact to be accounted for. We must ask how books that seem to be right in so many other respects could yet be in error at the crucial point of their self-awareness. Second, there is the testimony of Jesus. His testimony is the greatest argument of all. For even if Jesus were only a great teacher, his regard for the Bible as the ultimate authority in life could

68 The Sovereign God

hardly be disregarded. Third, there is the doctrinal and ethical superiority of the Bible to all other books. The Bible's superiority has often been acknowledged even by unbelievers and is denied by few who have actually read and studied its pages. Fourth, there is the power of the Bible to affect us as we read it. What produces such results if the Bible is not divine both in its source and its operation upon human lives?

Thomas Watson, one of the great English Puritans, wrote:
I wonder whence the Scriptures should come, if not from God. Bad men could not be the authors of it. Would their minds be employed in inditing such holy lines? Would they declare so fiercely against sin? Good men could not be the authors of it. Could they write in such a strain? or could it stand with their grace to counterfeit God's name, and put, Thus saith the Lord, *to a book of their own devising?*[1]

Here are four good reasons for regarding the Bible as the revealed Word of God, plus a fifth arising out of Watson's argument: the biblical writers would not have claimed divine origin for a book they knew to be purely their own. What follows are five more supports for the same conclusion.

The Unity in Diversity
A sixth reason for regarding the Bible as the revealed Word of God is the extraordinary unity of the book. This is an old argument, but it is a good one nonetheless. It is one that grows in force the more one studies the documents. The Bible is composed of sixty-six parts, or books, written over a period of approximately fifteen hundred years (from about 1450 B.C. to about A.D. 90) by over forty different people. These people were not alike. They came from various levels of society and from diverse backgrounds. Some were kings. Others were statesmen, priests, prophets, a tax collector, a physician, a tentmaker, fishermen. If asked about any subject at all, they would have had views as diverse as the opinions of people living today. Yet together they produced a volume that is a

marvelous unity in its doctrine, historical viewpoints, ethics and expectations. It is, in short, a single story of divine redemption begun in Israel, centered in Jesus Christ and culminating at the end of history.

The nature of this unity is important. To begin with, as R. A. Torrey notes,

It is not a superficial unity, but a profound unity. On the surface, we often find apparent discrepancy and disagreement, but, as we study, the apparent discrepancy and disagreement disappear, and the deep underlying unity appears. The more deeply we study, the more complete do we find the unity to be. The unity is also an organic one—that is, it is not the unity of a dead thing, like a stone, but of a living thing, like a plant. In the early books of the Bible we have the germinant thought; as we go on we have the plant, and further on the bud, and then the blossom, and then the ripened fruit. In Revelation we find the ripened fruit of Genesis. [2]

What can account for this unity? There is only one way of accounting for it: behind the efforts of the more than forty human authors is the one perfect, sovereign and guiding mind of God.

Uncanny Accuracy

A seventh reason for believing the Bible to be the Word of God is its uncommon accuracy. To be sure, its accuracy does not prove the Bible to be divine—human beings are also sometimes quite accurate—but it is what we should expect if the Bible is the result of God's effort. On the other hand, if the accuracy of the Bible extends to the point of inerrancy (which we will consider in the next chapter), that would be a direct proof of its divinity. For, although error is human, inerrancy is certainly divine.

At some points the accuracy of the Bible may be tested *externally,* as in the historical portions of the New Testament. We may take the Gospel of Luke and the book of Acts as an example. Luke/Acts is an attempt to write an "orderly ac-

count" of Jesus' life and of the rapid expansion of the early
Christian church (Lk. 1:1-4; Acts 1:1-2). That would be an
enormous undertaking even in our day. It was especially so in
ancient times when there were no newspapers or reference
books. In fact there were few written documents of any kind.
Yet in spite of this Luke charted the growth of what began as
an insignificant religious movement in a far corner of the
Roman empire, a movement that progressed quietly and without official sanction so that within forty years of the death
and resurrection of Jesus Christ there were Christian congre-
gations in most of the major cities of the empire. Does Luke's
work succeed? It does so remarkably and with what is apparently total accuracy.

For one thing, both books show amazing accuracy in handling official titles and corresponding spheres of influence.
This has been documented by F. F. Bruce of the University of
Manchester, England, in a small work entitled *The New Testament Documents: Are They Reliable?* Bruce writes:

> *One of the most remarkable tokens of his [Luke's] accuracy is his
> sure familiarity with the proper titles of all the notable persons
> who are mentioned in his pages. This was by no means such an easy
> feat in his days as it is in ours, when it is so simple to consult con-
> venient books of reference. The accuracy of Luke's use of the various
> titles in the Roman empire has been compared to the easy and con-
> fident way in which an Oxford man in ordinary conversation will
> refer to the Heads of colleges by their proper titles—the* Provost
> *of Oriel, the* Master *of Billiol, the* Rector *of Exeter, the* President
> *of Magdalen, and so on. A non-Oxonian like the present writer
> never feels quite at home with the multiplicity of these Oxford titles.* [3]

Luke obviously feels at home witn the Roman titles; he never
gets them wrong.

Bruce adds that Luke had a further difficulty in that the
titles often did not remain the same for any great length of
time. For example, the administration of a province might
pass from a direct representative of the emperor to a sena-

torial government, and would then be governed by a pro-consul rather than an imperial legate (*legatus pro praetore*). Cyprus, an imperial province until 22 B.C., became a sena-torial province in that year and was therefore no longer governed by an imperial legate but by a proconsul. Thus when Paul and Barnabas arrived in Cyprus about A.D. 47, it was the proconsul Sergius Paulus who greeted them (Acts 13:7).

Similarly, Achaia was a senatorial province from 27 B.C. to A.D. 15, and again subsequent to A.D. 44. Hence, Luke refers to Gallio, the Roman ruler in Greece, as "the proconsul of Achaia" (Acts 18:12), the title of the Roman representative during the time of Paul's visit to Corinth but not during the twenty-nine years prior to A.D. 44.[4]

This kind of accuracy by only one of the biblical writers is a testimony that may be multiplied almost indefinitely. For ex-ample, in Acts 19:38, the town clerk of Ephesus tries to calm the rioting citizens by referring them to the Roman authori-ties. "There are proconsuls," he says, using the plural. At first glance the writer seems to have made a mistake, since there was only one Roman proconsul in a given area at a time. But an examination shows that shortly before the rioting at Ephesus, Junius Silanus, the proconsul, had been murdered by messengers from Agrippina, the mother of the adolescent Nero. Since the new proconsul had not arrived in Ephesus, the town clerk's vagueness may be intentional or may even refer to the two emissaries, Helius and Celer, who were the apparent successors to Silanus's power. Luke captures the tone of the city in a time of internal disturbance, just as else-where he captures the tones of Antioch, Jerusalem, Rome and other cities, each of which had its own unique flavor.

Archaeology has also substantiated an extraordinary relia-bility for the writings of Luke and for other biblical docu-ments. A plaque has been found in Delphi identifying Gallio as the proconsul in Corinth at the precise time of Paul's visit to the city. The pool of Bethesda, containing five porticoes, has been found approximately seventy feet below the present level of the city of Jerusalem. It is mentioned in John 5:2, but it had been lost to view from the destruction of the city by the armies of Titus in A.D. 70 until recent times. The Pavement of Judgment, *Gabbatha,* mentioned in John 19:13, has also been uncovered.

Ancient documents—from Dura, Ras Shamra, Egypt and the Dead Sea—have thrown light on biblical reliability. In very recent years reports have been received of remarkable finds at Tell Mardikh in northwest Syria, the site of ancient Ebla. Thus far, fifteen thousand tablets dating from approximately 2300 B.C. (two to five hundred years before Abraham) have been discovered. In them are hundreds of names such as Abram, Israel, Esau, David, Yahweh and Jerusalem, showing these to be common names prior to their appearance in the biblical accounts. As they are studied carefully, these tablets will undoubtedly throw much light upon customs in the subsequent era of the Old Testament patriarchs, Moses, David and others. Their very existence already tends to verify the Old Testament narratives.

Internal evidence of the Bible's accuracy is also available, though not at all points. The reason is that parallel accounts of the same events are generally lacking. The Gospels do afford an example of internal evidence, particularly the accounts of the resurrection appearances of the Lord Jesus Christ. They are clearly four separate and independent accounts; otherwise there would be no apparent discrepancies. Writers working in collaboration would have cleared up any difficulties. Yet the Gospels don't really contradict each other. In all their major outlines they are mutually supportive. An incidental detail in one sometimes clarifies what seems to be a contradiction between two of the others.

Matthew speaks of Mary Magdalene and the "other" Mary as having gone to Christ's tomb on the first Easter morning. Mark mentions Mary Magdalene, Mary the mother of James (thus identifying Matthew's "other" Mary), and Salome. Luke mentions the two Marys, Joanna, and "the other women with them." John mentions only Mary Magdalene. On the surface these reports are different, but when they are examined further they reveal a remarkable harmony. Clearly a group of women, including all those mentioned, set out for the tomb. Finding the stone moved, the older women dispatched Mary Magdalene to tell the apostles of the disturbance and ask their advice. While she was gone the remaining women saw the angels (as Matthew, Mark and Luke report) but not the risen Lord, at least not until later. On the other hand, Mary, returning later and alone, did see him (as John discloses). In the same way, John's mention of "that other disciple" who accompanied Peter to the tomb throws light on Luke 24:24; that verse says that "some of those who were with us went to the tomb," after the women had been there, though Luke mentions only Peter (a singular individual) in his own narration.

These are little things, to be sure. But because they are little, they lend special weight to the impression of the Gospels' total accuracy.

Prophecy

An eighth reason for believing the Bible to be the Word of God is fulfilled prophecy. Here again is an extremely large subject, one clearly beyond the scope of this chapter. Nevertheless, it is possible to show briefly the general impact of the argument.

First, there are explicit prophecies. These concern the future of the Jewish people (including things that have already occurred and some that have not yet occurred) and the future of the gentile nations. Above all, many describe the coming of the Lord Jesus Christ, first to die and then afterward to return in power and great glory. Torrey cites five passages—Isaiah 53 (the entire chapter); Micah 5:2; Daniel 9: 25-27; Jeremiah 23:5-6; and Psalm 16:8-11—and comments:

In the passages cited we have predictions of a coming King of Israel. We are told the exact time of his manifestation to his people, the exact place of his birth, the family of which he should be born, the condition of the family at the time of his birth (a condition entirely different from that existing at the time the prophecy was written, and contrary to all the probabilities in the case), the manner of his reception by his people (a reception entirely different from that which would naturally be expected), the fact, method, and details regarding his death, with the specific circumstances regarding his burial, his resurrection subsequent to his burial, and his victory subsequent to his resurrection. These predictions were fulfilled with the most minute precision in Jesus of Nazareth.[5]

Another writer, E. Schuyler English, chairman of the editorial committee of *The New Scofield Reference Bible* (1967) and editor-in-chief of *The Pilgrim Bible* (1948), observes that

more than twenty Old Testament predictions relating to events that would surround the death of Christ, words written centuries before his first advent, were fulfilled with precision within a twenty-four-hour period at the time of his crucifixion [alone]. For example, in Matthew 27:35 it is written, "And they crucified him, and parted his garments, casting lots." This was in fulfillment of Psalm 22:18, where it is stated, "They part my garments among them, and cast lots upon my vesture."[6]

Many of these prophecies have been questioned, and attempts have been made to redate the Old Testament books, bringing them nearer to the time of Christ. But one can bring some prophecies to the very latest date imagined by the most radical and destructive critics, and they are still hundreds of years before the birth of Christ. Moreover, their cumulative witness is devastating. These are facts. They demand an accounting. What will account for them? The only fact that will account for such evidence is the existence of a sovereign God. He revealed in advance what would happen when he sent Jesus for the redemption of our race and then saw to it that such things actually took place.

Much more can be said in reference to prophecy. The preceding material relates only to the coming of Christ. There are also prophecies concerning the scattering and regathering of Israel as well as general and specific prophecies concerning the gentile nations and the capitals of those nations, many of which have been destroyed in precisely the way the Bible had indicated generations and even centuries before. The institutions, ceremonies, offerings and feasts of Israel are also prophetic of the life and ministry of Jesus.[7]

The Bible's Preservation

A ninth reason for believing the Bible to be the Word of God is its extraordinary preservation down through the centuries of Old Testament and church history. Today, after the Bible has been translated in part or whole into hundreds of languages, some with multiple versions, and after millions of copies of the sacred text have been printed and distributed, it would be a nearly impossible feat to destroy the Bible. But these conditions did not always prevail.

Until the time of the Reformation the biblical text was preserved by the laborious and time-consuming process of copying it over and over again by hand, at first onto papyrus sheets and then onto parchments. Throughout much of this time the Bible was an object of extreme hatred by many in authority. They tried to stamp it out. In the early days of the church, Celsus, Porphyry and Lucien tried to destroy it by arguments. Later the emperors Diocletian and Julian tried to destroy it by force. At several points it was actually a capital offense to possess a copy of parts of Holy Writ. Yet the text survived.

If the Bible had been only the thoughts and work of human beings it would have been eliminated long ago in the face of such opposition, as other books have been. But it has endured, fulfilling the words of Jesus, who said, "Heaven and earth will pass away, but my words will not pass away" (Mt. 24: 35).

Changed Lives

A tenth reason for believing the Bible to be the Word of God is its demonstrated ability to transform even the worst men and women, making them a blessing to their families, friends and community. The Bible speaks of this power: "The law of the LORD is perfect, reviving the soul; the testimony of the LORD is sure, making wise the simple; the precepts of the LORD are right, rejoicing the heart; the commandment of the LORD is pure, enlightening the eyes; the fear of the LORD is clean, enduring for ever; the ordinances of the LORD are true, and righteous altogether" (Ps. 19:7-9). As discussed in the last chapter, the transformation takes place by the power of the Holy Spirit who works through the Word.

Does the Bible actually transform men and women, turning them into godly persons? It does. Prostitutes have been reformed. Drunkards have become sober. Those filled with pride have become humble. Dishonest people have become people of integrity. Weak women and men have become strong, and all because of the transformation wrought in them by God as they have heard and studied the Scriptures.

A remarkable illustration comes from the life of Dr. Harry A. Ironside. Early in his ministry the great evangelist and Bible teacher was living in the San Francisco Bay area working with a group of believers called "Brethren." One Sunday as he was walking through the city he came upon a group of Salvation Army workers holding a meeting on the corner of Market and Grant Avenues. There were probably sixty of them. When they recognized Ironside they immediately asked him if he would give his testimony. So he did, giving a word about how God had saved him through faith in the bodily death and literal resurrection of Jesus.

As he was speaking, Ironside noticed that on the edge of the crowd a well-dressed man had taken a card from his pocket and had written something on it. As Ironside finished his talk this man came forward, lifted his hat and very politely handed him the card. On one side was his name, which Ironside immediately recognized. The man was one of the early socialists who had made a name for himself lecturing not only for socialism but also against Christianity. As Ironside turned the card over, he read, "Sir, I challenge you to debate with me the question 'Agnosticism versus Christianity' in the Academy of Science Hall next Sunday afternoon at four o'clock. I will pay all expenses."

Ironside reread the card aloud and then replied somewhat like this. "I am very much interested in this challenge. . . . Therefore I will be glad to agree to this debate on the following conditions: namely, that in order to prove that Mr. _____ has something worth fighting for and worth debating about, he will promise to bring with him to the Hall next Sunday two people whose qualifications I will give in a moment, as proof that agnosticism is of real value in changing human lives and building true character.

"First, he must promise to bring with him one man who was for years what we commonly call a 'down-and-outer.' I am not particular as to the exact nature of the sins that had wrecked his life and made him an outcast from society—whether a drunkard, or a criminal of some kind, or a victim of his sensual appetite—but a man who for years was under the power of evil habits from which he could not deliver himself, but who on some occasion entered one of Mr. _____'s meetings and heard his glorification of agnosticism and his denunciations of the Bible and Christianity, and whose heart and mind as he listened to such an address were so deeply stirred that he went away from that meeting saying, 'Henceforth, I too am an agnostic!' and as a result of imbibing that particular philosophy found that a new power had come into his life. The sins he once loved he now hates, and righteousness and goodness are now the ideals of his life. He is now an entirely new man, a credit to himself and an asset to society—all because he is an agnostic.

"Secondly, I would like Mr. _____ to promise to bring with him one woman—and I think he may have more difficulty in finding the woman than the man—who was once a poor, wrecked, characterless outcast, the slave of evil passions, and the victim of man's corrupt living ... perhaps one who had lived for years in some evil resort, ... utterly lost, ruined and wretched because of her life of sin. But this woman also entered a hall where Mr. _____ was loudly proclaiming his agnosticism and ridiculing the message of the Holy Scriptures. As she listened, hope was born in her heart, and she said, 'This is just what I need to deliver me from the slavery of sin!' She followed the teaching and became an intelligent agnostic or infidel. As a result, her whole being revolted against the degradation of the life she had been living. She fled from the den of iniquity where she had been held captive so long; and today, rehabilitated, she has won her way back to an honored position in society and is living a clean, virtuous, happy life—all because she is an agnostic.

"Now," he said, addressing the gentleman who had presented him with his card and the challenge, "if you will promise to bring these two people with you as examples of what agnosticism can do, I will promise to meet you at the Hall of Science at four o'clock next Sunday, and I will bring with me at the very least 100 men and women who for years lived in just such sinful degradation as I have tried to depict, but who have been gloriously saved through believing the gospel which you ridicule. I will have these men and women with me on the platform as witnesses to the miraculous saving power of Jesus Christ and as present-day proof of the truth of the Bible."

Dr. Ironside then turned to the Salvation Army captain, a woman, and said, "Captain, have you any who could go with me to such a meeting?"

She exclaimed with enthusiasm, "We can give you forty at least just from this one corps, and we will give you a brass band to lead the procession!"

"Fine," Dr. Ironside answered. "Now, Mr. _____, I will have no difficulty in picking up sixty others from the various missions, gospel halls, and evangelical churches of the city; and if you will promise faithfully to bring two such exhibits as I have described, I will come marching in at the head of such a procession, with the band playing 'Onward, Christian Soldiers,' and I will be ready for the debate."

Apparently the man who had made the challenge must have had some sense of humor, for he smiled wryly and waved his hand in a deprecating kind of way as if to say, "Nothing doing!" and then edged out of the crowd while the bystanders clapped for Ironside and the others.[8]

The power of the living Christ operating by means of the Holy Spirit through the written Word changes lives. This has been true throughout church history. It is true in our own time also. It is a powerful proof that the Bible is indeed the Word of God.

6 HOW TRUE IS THE BIBLE?

From the beginning of the Christian church until well into the eighteenth century the vast majority of Christians of all denominations acknowledged that the Scriptures of the Old and New Testaments were uniquely the Word of God. In these books God speaks. And because God speaks in Scripture—as he does nowhere else in the same way—all who claimed to be Christians recognized the Bible as a divine authority binding upon all, a body of objective truth that transcends subjective understanding. In these books God's saving acts in history are told to human beings so that we might believe. And the events of that history are divinely interpreted that men and women might understand the gospel and respond to it intelligently both in thought and action. The Bible is the written Word of God. Because the Bible is the Word of God, the Scriptures of the Old and New Testaments are authoritative and inerrant.

Early Christianity

There are many statements to substantiate the existence of this high view of Scripture in the documents of the early church. Irenaeus, who lived and wrote in Lyon in the early years of the second century, wrote that we should be "most properly assured that the Scriptures are indeed perfect, since they were spoken by the Word of God and His Spirit."[1] Cyril of Jerusalem, who lived in the fourth century, said, "Not even a casual statement must be delivered without the Holy Scriptures; nor must we be drawn aside by mere probability and artifices of speech. . . . For this salvation which we believe depends not on ingenious reasoning, but on demonstration of the Holy Scriptures."[2]

In a letter to Jerome, the translator of the Latin Vulgate, Augustine said, "I . . . believe most firmly that not one of those authors had erred in writing anything at all. If I do find anything in those books which seems contrary to truth, I decide that either the text is corrupt, or the translator did not follow what was really said, or that I failed to understand it. . . . The canonical books are entirely free of falsehood."[3] And in his treatise "On the Trinity" he warns, "Do not be willing to yield to my writings as to the canonical Scriptures; but in these, when thou hast discovered even what thou didst not previously believe, believe it unhesitatingly."[4]

The same position holds for Luther. Some hold that Luther's reference to the Bible as "the cradle of Christ proves that he believed in a revelation within the Bible (not one that was identical with it) and that he held the Scriptures in less esteem than the Christ they speak of. For some this means that not all the Bible is the Word of God. But this is not right.

Luther's phrase, the "cradle of Christ," occurs at the end of the third paragraph of his "Preface to the Old Testament." And there, as the late Lutheran scholar J. Theodore Mueller has demonstrated, Luther is actually defending the value of the Old Testament for Christians. Far from deprecating

Scripture, Luther is actually concerned "to express his most reverent esteem of Holy Scripture, which offers to man the supreme blessing of eternal salvation in Christ."[5] Luther himself says, "I beg and faithfully warn every pious Christian not to be offended by the simplicity of the language and the stories that will often meet him here [in the Old Testament]. Let him not doubt that, however simple they may seem, they are the very words, works, judgments, and deeds of the high majesty, power, and wisdom of God."[6]

In another place Luther says, "The Scriptures, although they also were written by men, are not of men nor from men, but from God."[7] Again, "We must make a great difference between God's Word and the word of man. A man's word is a little sound, that flies into the air, and soon vanishes; but the Word of God is greater than heaven and earth, yea, greater than death and hell, for it forms part of the power of God, and endures everlastingly."[8]

In some places Calvin is even more outspoken. Commenting on 2 Timothy 3:16, the Geneva reformer maintains,

This is the principle that distinguishes our religion from all others, that we know that God hath spoken to us and are fully convinced that the prophets did not speak of themselves, but as organs of the Holy Spirit uttered only that which they had been commissioned from heaven to declare. All those who wish to profit from the Scriptures must first accept this as a settled principle, that the Law and the prophets are not teachings handed on at the pleasure of men, or produced by men's minds as their source, but are dictated by the Holy Spirit.

He concludes, "We owe to the Scripture the same reverence as we owe to God, since it has its only source in Him and has nothing of human origin mixed with it."[9] In his comments on the Psalms he speaks of the Bible as that "certain and unerring rule" (Ps. 5:11).

John Wesley says the same. "The Scripture, therefore, is a rule sufficient in itself, and was by men divinely inspired at once delivered to the world."[10] "If there be any mistakes in the Bible, there may well be a thousand. If there be one falsehood in that book, it did not come from the God of truth."[11]

It was the glory of the church that in the first sixteen or seventeen centuries all Christians in every place, despite their differences of opinion on theology or on questions of church order, exhibited at least a mental allegiance to the Bible as the supreme and inerrant authority for the Christian in all matters. It might be neglected. There might be disagreements about what it actually teaches. It might even be contradicted. Still it was the Word of God. It was the only infallible rule of faith and practice.

Age of Decline
In the post-Reformation period the orthodox view of Scripture came under increasingly devastating attacks. In the Roman Catholic Church the attacks came from the Church's established traditions. Already weakened by centuries of appealing to the early church fathers rather than to the Scripture in defense of a point of doctrine and in violent reaction to the Protestant Reformation, the Roman Catholic Church in 1546 took the step of officially placing the tradition of the Church alongside Scripture as an equally valid source of revelation. The full significance of that decision was doubtlessly overlooked at the time of the Council of Trent, but it was monumental. The act had tragic consequences for the Roman Catholic Church, as the continuing development of debilitating doctrines, such as Mariology and the veneration of the saints, indicates. In theory, the Bible remains inerrant, at least for large sectors of Catholicism. But the deep human preference for traditions rather than an absolute and inerrant Word inevitably shifts the balance of authority away from God's Word.

In Protestantism the attack came from the so-called higher criticism. For a time, as the result of their heritage and sharp polemic against Catholicism, Protestant churches generally held to an infallible Bible. But in the eighteenth and particularly in the nineteenth century a critical appraisal of the Scriptures, backed by a naturalistic rationalism, succeeded in dislodging the Bible from the place it had held previously. For the church of the age of rationalism, the Bible became man's word about God and man rather than God's word to man. Eventually, having rejected the unique, divine character of the Bible, many critics rejected its authority also.

The Catholic Church weakened the orthodox view of the Bible by exalting human traditions to the stature of Scripture. Protestants weakened the orthodox view of Scripture by lowering the Bible to the level of traditions. The differences are great, but the results were similar. Neither group entirely denied the revelational quality of Scripture. But in both cases the unique character of Scripture was lost, its authority forfeited and the function of the Bible as the reforming voice of God within the church forgotten.

The fact that neither of these two positions is tenable should be evident to everyone and should push the church back toward its original position. But this does not seem to be happening. Instead, some evangelicals who have traditionally insisted on an inerrant Word seem to be moving in a more liberal direction, displaying an increasingly ambivalent attitude toward infallibility.

We must be extremely careful at this point. There is value in questioning what we should mean by "inerrancy," which differs from outright and dangerous rejection of it. For example, some very conservative scholars have asked whether *inerrancy* is really the best term to use in reference to the Bible since it would seem to demand a precision of detail so exact as to include even a need for faultless grammar, which does not exist. They have preferred the word *infallibility* at this point. Others have faulted the term *inerrancy* for seeming to require modern, scientific standards of accuracy in expression which the ancient writers obviously did not have. Such scholars have preferred to speak of the Bible as *trustworthy* or *truthful*. But these are not the areas of real concern. In these areas there may well be movement, based on the knowledge that no one term—*inerrancy, infallibility, trustworthiness, reliability, truthfulness,* or others—perfectly describes what we mean. But there must not be movement in holding to the unique character and authority of the Bible, in whole and in part, as the Word of God. The word *inerrancy,* whatever its limitations, at least preserves this emphasis.

What Is the Issue?

Modern biblical criticism is generally credited with bringing down the old inerrancy view. It is said that inerrancy was a possible option in days when men and women knew very little about the biblical texts or biblical history. But modern discoveries have changed all that. Today we know that the Bible contains errors, so we are told, and therefore the overthrow of biblical infallibility is a *fait accompli.* For example, Quirinius was apparently "not strictly" the governor of Syria at the time of Christ's birth (Lk. 2:2). Moses "did not" write the Pentateuch. One scholar wrote, "The scientific development of the last century has rendered untenable the whole conception of the Bible as a verbally inspired book, to which we can appeal with absolute certainty for infallible guidance in all matters of faith and conduct."[12]

But does modern critical study demand radical change of our view of Scripture? Doubts emerge when we realize that most of the alleged errors in the Bible are not recent discoveries, due to scientific criticism, but are only difficulties known centuries ago to most serious biblical students. Origen, Augustine, Luther, Calvin and countless others were aware of the problems. They knew that various biblical time periods are reported differently by different writers. (For example Genesis 15:13 says the duration of the bondage of Israel in

Egypt was four hundred years while Exodus 12:41 says it was four hundred and thirty years.) They knew details of parallel narrations sometimes vary (as in the number of angels at the tomb of Christ following the resurrection). But they understood these to result merely from the authors' varying perspectives or specific intent in writing. They did not feel compelled to jettison the orthodox conception of Scripture because of these problems.

The real problem with inerrancy therefore goes beyond the data produced by scientific criticism to the philosophy underlying the modern critical enterprise. That philosophy is naturalism. This world view denies the supernatural, or it seeks to place it beyond scientific investigation. The supernatural therefore has no direct correlation with the specific words of the biblical text. It is, to use Francis Schaeffer's term, an "upper story" reality, beyond proof or contradiction. Thus, writes Pinnock,

Negative criticism is now the tool of the new theology. It is no longer employed in a hit-and-run way to ferret out objectionable features of biblical teaching. It now serves to discredit the entire notion at the heart of Christianity that there is a body of revealed information, normative for Christian theology. In the modern interest in hermeneutics we see no revival of concern to take Scriptural truth seriously, but only an attempt to use the Bible in a new, non-literal, existential way. [13]

A prime example of this would be the theology of Rudolf Bultmann, who writes volumes of theological exposition but who denies that Christian revelation possesses propositional content at all.

If that is the real issue in the inerrancy debate, then the debate is obviously far more important than whether or not a few insignificant errors can be shown to exist in the Scriptures. What is at stake is the whole matter of revelation. Can God reveal himself to humanity? And, to be more specific, can he reveal himself in language, the specifics of which become normative for Christian faith and action? With an inerrant Bible these things are possible. Without it, theology inevitably enters a wasteland of human speculation. The church, which needs a sure Word of God, flounders. Without an inerrant revelation, theology is not only adrift, it is meaningless. Having repudiated its right to speak of Scripture on the basis of Scripture, it forfeits its right to speak at all.

The Case for Inerrancy

Divine truthfulness is the rock beneath a defense of Scripture as the authoritative and entirely trustworthy Word of God. The steps in the defense are as follows:

1. The Bible is a generally trustworthy document. Its reliability is established by treating it like any other historical record like, for instance, the works of Josephus or the accounts of war by Julius Caesar.

2. On the basis of the history recorded by the Bible we have sufficient reason for believing that the central character of the Bible, Jesus Christ, did what he is claimed to have done and therefore is who he claimed to be: the unique Son of God.

3. As the unique Son of God, the Lord Jesus Christ is an infallible authority.

4. Jesus Christ not only assumed the Bible's authority; he taught it, going so far as to teach that it is entirely without error and is eternal, being the Word of God. "For truly, I say to you, till heaven and earth pass away, not an iota, not a dot, will pass from the law until all is accomplished" (Mt. 5:18).

5. If the Bible is the Word of God, as Jesus taught, it must for this reason alone be entirely trustworthy and inerrant, for God is a God of truth.

6. Therefore, on the basis of the teaching of Jesus Christ, the infallible Son of God, the church believes the Bible also to be infallible.[14]

In other words, the case for inerrancy rests upon and is an inevitable consequence of the type of material presented in chapters 3—4. The Bible as a historical document gives us reliable knowledge of an infallible Christ. Christ gives the highest regard to Scripture. Consequently, the doctrines of Christ should and must be the doctrines of his followers.

The Case against Inerrancy

Many who follow the logic of the traditional defense of the inerrancy of Scripture are nevertheless bothered by what seem to be insurmountable objections. Let's look at these objections and see whether they are as formidable as they appear.

The first objection is based upon the *character of the biblical texts.* "Granted," someone might say, "that these are reliable historical documents; isn't it true, nevertheless, that this is precisely one of the problems? They are obviously historical and therefore human documents. They are selective in what they contain. They use the limited, sometimes figurative language of the age in which they were written. Parallel accounts reveal different points of view possessed by the different authors. The literary polish of the material varies. Is that what we are to expect of a divine revelation? Doesn't this in itself mean that we are dealing with a purely human book?"

It isn't up to us, however, to say in what form a divine revelation must be given nor to insist that the revelation cannot be divine because of certain characteristics. Obviously, nothing human is a fit vehicle for God's truth. But God is not prevented from stooping to use human language to convey his truth inerrantly. Calvin compared God's action to that of a mother who uses baby talk in communicating with a child. It is obviously a limited communication, for the child cannot converse on the mother's level. But it is true communication nonetheless. Therefore the character of the documents in itself has nothing to do with the inerrancy question.

A second objection to inerrancy begins where the first objection leaves off. It deals not so much with the character of the biblical books but with the simple fact that they are *obviously human productions.* "To err is human," such critics maintain. "Consequently, the Bible, as a human book, must contain errors."

At first glance this argument may appear logical, but further examination shows that it is not necessarily so. While human beings do err, it is not true that a given individual will err all the time or in any case necessarily. For example, the development of a scientific equation is, for the purpose for which it is given, literally infallible. The same can be said for a correctly printed announcement of a meeting, instructions for operating a car and other things. "To be sure," as John Warwick Montgomery notes in developing this argument, "the production over centuries of sixty-six inerrant and mutually consistent books by different authors is a tall order—and we cheerfully appeal to God's Spirit to achieve it—but the point remains that there is nothing metaphysically inhuman or against human nature in such a possibility."[15]

The analogy between the conception and birth of the Lord Jesus Christ and the giving of our Bible is instructive. We read that, when the Lord was conceived in the womb of the virgin Mary, the Holy Spirit overshadowed her so that the child that was born was called "the Son of God" (Lk. 1:35). The divine and the human met in Christ's conception, and the result was also in its turn both human and divine. Christ was a real man. He was a particular person, a Jew. He had a certain measurable weight and a recognizable appearance. You could have taken a picture of him. Still he was also God Almighty and without sin.

Somewhat comparably, just as the Holy Spirit came upon the virgin Mary so that she conceived the human Son of God in her womb, so also did the Holy Spirit come upon the brain cells of Moses, David, the prophets, the evangelists, Paul and the other biblical writers, so that they brought forth from their minds those books which constitute our Bible. Their writings bear the marks of human personality. They differ in style. Yet the ultimate source is divine, and the touch of the human does not stamp them with error any more than the womb of Mary imparted sin to the Savior.

A third objection to inerrancy is based on the fact that *inerrancy is claimed only for the original autographs,* not the copies that have been made from them upon which our contemporary translations are based. Since no one living has ever seen the autographs and we are therefore unable either to verify or falsify the claim, is it not epistemological nonsense to appeal to them? "So what if there is an inerrant original?" someone might argue. "Since we don't have it, the appeal to an inerrant Bible is meaningless."

But is it? It would be if two things were true: (1) if the number of apparent errors remained constant as one moved back through the copies toward the original writing and (2) if believers in infallibility appealed to an original that differed substantially from the best manuscript copies in existence. But neither is the case. On the contrary,

> the number of textual errors steadily diminishes as one moves back in the direction of the lost autographs, reasonably encouraging the supposition that could we entirely fill in the interval between the originals and our earliest texts and fragments (some New Testament papyri going back to the first century itself), all apparent errors would disappear.... The conservative evangelical only appeals to the missing autographs over against existent best texts in those limited and specific instances (such as the recording of numerals) where independent evidence shows a very high probability of transcriptional errors from the very outset.[16]

The believer in infallibility handles textual problems in the same way that a secular scholar handles problems relating to any ancient document. However, due to the extraordinary number and variety of the biblical manuscripts, there is no reason to doubt that today's text is identical to the original text in all but a few places. And these few are clearly known to commentators.

A fourth major objection to the doctrine of inerrancy concerns the proper *function of language as a vehicle of truth.* Some scholars imply that truth transcends language so that the truth of Scripture is to be found in the thoughts of Scripture rather than in its words. But does that make sense? "To accept the inspiration of the thoughts and not the words of the biblical writers runs counter not only to the Scriptural claims, but is intrinsically meaningless," as Pinnock observes. "What is an inspired thought expressed in uninspired language?"[17] If the Bible is inspired at all, it must be inspired verbally. And verbal inspiration means infallibility.

To be sure, there are parts of Scripture where the choice of a word may make very little difference in recording a fact of doctrine. The wording of some verses can be changed, as translators regularly do to convey the proper meaning to a particular culture. But there are other places where the words are crucial, and a doctrine will inevitably suffer if we fail to take them seriously. Certainly, if we are to have an authoritative Bible, we must also have a verbally inspired and therefore an infallible Bible, a Bible that is infallible at the point in question and at other points as well. This view agrees with the Bible's own teaching and with the nature of language.

Are There Errors?

Finally, there are those who would follow the argument so far, and even agree with it in places, but who, nevertheless, feel that certain "errors" have been disclosed by the "assured results" of biblical scholarship. Are there errors that have really been proven to exist? There are difficulties in places. No one questions that. But has scholarship actually demonstrated that the books of the Bible are fallible and therefore written only by men after all?

There was a time not long ago when claims such as these

were made by many influential people and were made quite openly. In past years almost every biblical theologian and scholar spoke of so-called certain results or assured findings that were imagined to have laid the orthodox conception of the Bible to rest forever. Today, however, as anyone who has had the opportunity to delve deeply into such questions knows, these phrases no longer occur with such frequency. In fact, they hardly occur at all. Why? Simply because, as a result of a continuing march of biblical and archaeological investigations, many so-called assured results have blown up in the faces of those who propounded them.

In 2 Kings 15:29 there is a reference to a king of Assyria named Tiglath-Pileser. He is spoken of as having conquered the Israelites of the northern kingdom and as having taken many of them into captivity. A generation ago scholars were saying—their books are still in our libraries—that this king never existed and that the account of the fall of Israel to Assyria is something akin to mythology. Now, however, archaeologists have excavated Tiglath-Pileser's capital city and can give his history. They have even found his name pressed into bricks which read: "I, Tiglath-Pileser, king of the west lands, king of the earth, whose kingdom extends to the great sea. . . ." The English reader can find accounts of his battles with Israel in James B. Pritchard's volume *Ancient Near Eastern Texts Relating to the Old Testament.* About the same time, some scholars were denying that Moses could have written the first five books of the Bible on the grounds, which seemed irrefutable enough, that writing had not been invented in his day. Since that time, however, archaeologists have unearthed thousands of tablets and inscriptions written many hundreds of years before Moses and even before Abraham. In fact, they now know of six different written languages from or before Moses' period.

In more recent days many could be found who denied that the historical books of the New Testament were written close enough to the events they relate to be reliable. The Synoptic Gospels (Matthew, Mark and Luke) in particular were dated late; and John, which seemed to have the greatest measure of Greek flavoring, was pushed back well into the second or, by some scholars, into the third Christian century. In time, however, a piece of papyrus was uncovered in Egypt which required scholars to date the fourth Gospel no later than the year A.D. 125 and presumably much before that time.

The results of scholarship, far from discrediting the Bible, actually increasingly validate its claims. They do not prove infallibility—no amount of data alone can do that—but they do lead in the direction of reliability. They reveal nothing incompatible with the highest view of Scripture. In fact, as *Time* magazine acknowledged in a 1974 cover story on the Bible,

> *The breadth, sophistication and diversity of all this biblical investigation are impressive, but it begs a question: Has it made the Bible more credible or less? Literalists who feel the ground move when a verse is challenged would have to say that credibility has suffered. Doubt has been sown, faith is in jeopardy. But believers who expect something else from the Bible may well conclude that its credibility has been enhanced. After more than two centuries of facing the heaviest scientific guns that could be brought to bear, the Bible has survived—and is perhaps the better for the siege. Even on the critics' own terms—historical fact—the Scriptures seem more acceptable now than they did when the rationalists began the attack.* [18]

Standing on the Rock

The Christian need never fear to stand on the Word of God, recognizing its full authority as the Lord Jesus Christ himself did. At times there will be critical theories that run against it. The arguments may seem unanswerable, so much so that the one who tries to stand against them may be dismissed as an obscurantist. The wise of this world will say, "You can believe that if you want to, but the results of scientific criticism teach us better." Such things have happened before and will happen again. But Christians who will stand on Scripture will find even within their lifetime that, as the so-called assured results begin to crumble around the scholars, the view of the Bible held by the Lord Jesus Christ, the historical view of the church, will prevail.

A number of years ago a former leader of the Church of England, Bishop Ryle of Liverpool, wrote, "Give me the plenary, verbal theory of biblical inspiration with all its difficulties, rather than the doubt. I accept the difficulties and humbly wait for their solution. But while I wait, I am standing on the rock."

7 MODERN BIBLICAL CRITICISM

Modern biblical criticism more than anything else has weakened and almost destroyed the high view of the Bible previously held throughout Christendom. Thus it is necessary to look at the main lines of this criticism as it has developed in the last two centuries and then reflect on it from an evangelical perspective.

A Recent Movement

Higher criticism of the Old and New Testaments along literary lines is not in itself peculiar to the nineteenth and twentieth centuries. Theodore of Mopsuestia, one of the most noted theologians of the Antiochian school, relegated a number of the psalms (such as 51, 65 and 127) to the age of the Exile. During the Middle Ages, Ibn Ezra, a Jewish scholar, claimed to have discovered a number of anachronisms in the Pentateuch. Even Martin Luther applied a form of literary criticism in his occasional pronouncements about the authenticity and relative value of the biblical books. Nevertheless, it was not until the middle of the eighteenth century, 1753, to be exact, that higher criticism was introduced on a scale and with a purpose comparable to our use of the phrase today.

In that year a scientist and physician in the French court, Jean Astruc, published a work on the literary sources of Genesis and set forth a method of biblical study which was to find widespread acceptance, first in Germany, then throughout Europe and the United States. Astruc observed that

in the Hebrew text of Genesis, God is designated by two different names. The first is Elohim, for, while this name has other meanings in Hebrew, it is especially applied to the Supreme Being. The other is Jehovah . . . the great name of God, expressing his essence. Now one might suppose that the two names were used indiscriminately as synonymous terms, merely to lend variety to the style. This, however, would be in error. The names are never intermixed; there are whole chapters, or large parts of chapters, in which God is always called Elohim, and others, at least as numerous, in which he is always named Jehovah. If Moses were the author of Genesis, we should have to ascribe this strange and harsh variation to himself. But can we conceive such negligence in the composition of so short a book as Genesis? Shall we impute to Moses a fault such as no other writer has committed? Is it not more natural to explain this variation by supposing that Genesis was composed of two or three memoirs, the authors of which gave different names to God, one using Elohim, another that of Jehovah or Jehovah Elohim?[1]

Astruc's statement is a primitive expression of the critical spirit; it reveals characteristics that were soon to become representative of literary criticism at large. First, it reveals a break with traditional views, according to which Moses was the author of the Pentateuch. Second, it discloses a shift in the object of study, from the simple meaning of the words themselves to questions of the authenticity and integrity of the biblical books. Third, it displays a new method of procedure. By laying aside the testimony of history and tradition, at least temporarily, this criticism focuses upon the style, vocabulary, syntax, ideas and features of the documents as the sole basis upon which questions concerning authenticity and integrity may be answered.

At first Astruc's work received little notice. Yet within a few years it was picked up by some German scholars and others and was expanded to include the whole Old Testament. Johann Eichhorn applied Astruc's approach to the entire Pentateuch. Wilhelm De Wette and Edward Reuss attempted to bring the results into line with Jewish history. Reuss concluded that in the correct historical sequence the prophets are earlier than the law and the psalms later than both. The most popular and, in some sense, the culminating work in this field was the *Prolegomena* of Julius Wellhausen published in 1878. This work widely disseminated the four-stage documentary hypothesis known as JEPD. (*J* for the Jehovah source, *E* for the Elohim source, *P* for the priestly documents and code, and *D* for the later editorial work of the Deuteronomist or Deuteronomic school). Wellhausen dated the writing of the law after the Babylonian exile and placed only the Book of the Covenant and the most ancient editing of the J and E narrative sections prior to the eighth century B.C.

The profound change this involved is clear in the words of E. C. Blackman, who hails Wellhausen's achievement as making possible "the understanding of the Old Testament in terms of progressive revelation . . . a real liberation."[2] Emil G. Kraeling notes that it also "marked the beginning of a completely secular and evolutionistic study of the Old Testament sources."[3]

The Jesus of History

In New Testament studies the energies of the higher critics have been directed in a slightly different direction; namely, to recover the "Jesus of history" through a study of the origins of the Gospel narratives and the development of New Testament theology as preserved in the Epistles of Paul, the pastorals, the Johannine literature and Revelation. But the same principles are involved, and they have been carried forward in New Testament studies in an even more radical way than in the nineteenth-century investigation of the Pentateuch.

The origin of higher critical principles in New Testament study is usually traced to Ferdinand Christian Baur (1792-1860), who tried to organize the material along historical lines. Hegel had developed the theory that historical development proceeds by thesis, antithesis and synthesis. Baur applied Hegelian principles to biblical history, citing the supposed conflict of Petrine and Pauline theology as evidence of a doctrinal thesis and antithesis within the early church. In Baur's view, this led to the synthesis of early Catholicism. Today Baur's general thesis is rejected. Still he succeeded in shaking the traditional views concerning the authorship and composition of the New Testament books and called the attention of the scholarly world to a rediscovery of the historical Christ as the primary New Testament problem.

The so-called quest for the historical Jesus dates from the death in 1768 of Hermann Samuel Reimarus, the historian with whom Albert Schweitzer begins his survey of nineteenth-century research. Reimarus was no New Testament scholar, but at his death he left behind a manuscript that was to have far-reaching implications. He argued that historians must distinguish between the "aim" of Jesus and the "aim" of his disciples, that is, between the Jesus of history and the Christ of early Christian preaching. Faced with a choice between what he believed to be mutually exclusive aims, Reimarus opted for the former, positing a nonsupernatural Jesus. According to him, Jesus preached the coming of God's kingdom, but he died forsaken by God and disillusioned. Christianity was viewed as the product of early disciples who stole the corpse, proclaimed a bodily resurrection and gathered followers.

Reimarus was extreme and his work polemical. But his

views of Christian origins set the pattern for a century of historical-Jesus research. Reacting against the supernatural element in the Gospels and casting about for a Jesus made in their own image, idealists found Christ to be the ideal man; rationalists saw him as the great teacher of morality; and socialists viewed him as a friend of the poor and a revolutionary. The most popular "lives of Jesus," the two by David Friedrich Strauss, rejected most of the Gospel material as mythology; and Bruno Bauer ended his quest by denying that there ever was a historical Jesus. Bauer explained all the stories about Jesus as the products of the imagination of the primitive Christian community.

One can hardly fail to be impressed even today at the immense energy and talent that German scholars poured into the old quest for the "original" Jesus, but the results were meager and the conclusions wrong, as Schweitzer found in his study. Scholarship had attempted to modernize Jesus, but the Jesus they produced was neither the historical Jesus nor the Christ of Scripture.

Bultmann and Mythology
In more recent years, higher criticism of the New Testament has centered around the work of Rudolf Bultmann, former professor at the University of Marburg, Germany, the acknowledged father of form criticism. Much of Bultmann's energy was expended on stripping away what he feels to be the "mythology" of the New Testament writers: heaven, hell, miracles. But Bultmann's views are misunderstood if one imagines that the historically real Jesus lies beneath the mythological layer. According to Bultmann, what lies beneath the mythology is the church's deepest understanding of life created by its experience with the _risen_ Lord. Consequently, nothing may be known about Jesus in terms of pure history except the fact that he existed. In Bultmann's work, _Jesus and the Word,_ he states, "We can know almost nothing concern-

ing the life and personality of Jesus."[4]

Operating under the assumption that a period of oral transmission intervened between the years of Christ's earthly ministry and the transcribing of the traditions about him in the Gospels, Bultmann envisions a creative church, one that gradually superimposed its own world picture upon what it had received of the times and teachings of Jesus. The church's creativity took place in an "oral stage" in the development of the tradition. During this period much of the Gospel material circulated in the form of separate oral units, which may today be classified and arranged in a time sequence on the basis of their form. It is believed, by Bultmann and others of his school, that much may be inferred about the situation in the church from these Gospel "units." But virtually nothing may be learned about the actual, historical Jesus. The expressions of faith of the early church, preserved for us in the New Testament, must be reinterpreted in existential terms if they are to have meaning for the modern era.

In rejecting the supposed New Testament mythology, Bultmann rejects a literal pre-existence of Christ, his virgin birth, his sinlessness and deity, the value of his atoning death, a literal resurrection and ascension of Christ, and the future judgment of all people. They speak rather of a new "possibility of existence," meaning the possibility of letting go of the past (dying with Christ) and opening oneself to the future (rising with Christ). To embrace this possibility brings inner release and overwhelming freedom (salvation).

Lutheran scholar Edgar Krentz writes of Bultmann's conclusions,

> *On the one hand the Scriptures are, like any other book, the object of historical inquiry, which seeks the facts. But no absolute meaning is to be found in the facts. Meaning is to be found only as man personally confronts history and finds meaning for his own existence (existential interpretations). Only as man is not subjected to a strange world view is he set free to believe. It is this self-understand-*

ing that determines the work of interpretation, for interpretation must give free play for faith, God's creation.[5]

To summarize, according to the Bultmannian school: (1) the earliest Christian sources show no interest in the actual history or personality of Jesus, (2) the biblical documents are fragmentary and legendary, (3) there are no other sources against which the data provided by the biblical writers may be checked, and (4) preoccupation with the historical Jesus is actually destructive of Christianity, for it leads, not to faith in Jesus as God, but to a Jesus-cult, the effects of which can be clearly seen in pietism.

The weaknesses of some of these perspectives are now being seen in some quarters. Consequently, theological leadership is in the process of passing into other hands.[6]

Major Characteristics

Brief as it has been, our review of higher criticism reveals great diversity. Viewpoints are constantly changing, and even in the same period, those working in similar areas often contradict each other. However, in spite of the diversity, there are certain characteristics that tie the various expressions of the higher criticism together.

First, there is its *humanism.* In most forms of the modern debate the Scriptures of the Old and New Testaments are handled as if they are *man's word about God, rather than God's Word to man.* But this, as J. I. Packer points out, is simply the Romantic philosophy of religion set out by Friedrich Schleiermacher (1768-1834), "namely that the real subject matter of theology is not divinely revealed truths, but human religious experience."[7] Within this framework the Bible is only a record of human reflection and action in the field of religion. The interpreter's task becomes the work of sifting that experience out and evaluating it for possible use in our age.

It must be recognized of course, as was pointed out in an

earlier chapter, that the Bible does have a genuinely human element. On the other hand, we must object to any attempt to make it human at the expense of its being divine. Besides, as Packer adds,

> *If one factor must be stressed at the expense of the other, far less is lost by treating the Scriptures simply as the written oracles of God than simply as a collection of Jewish ideas about God. For we have no reason to regard merely human words as inerrant and authoritative; what will be authoritative for us, if we take the liberal view, is our own judgment as to how far they may be trusted and how far not. Thus, we land, willy-nilly, in subjectivism.*[8]

A clear example of such subjectivism is the section on "Scripture" from *The Common Catechism,* a widely advertised modern statement of faith by an impressive team of contemporary Catholic and Protestant theologians. It states:

> *Everything we will have to discuss ... is based on this now un-questioned assumption that the evidence of the Bible may and must be examined as evidence of the faith of a number of men and a number of generations. . . . For the future we can no longer say, "The Bible is the word of God." Even saying "The word of God is in the Bible" would be wrong, if it were taken to mean that one set of statements in the Bible were purely human words and the rest God's word. We must say something like: "The Bible is not God's word, but becomes God's word for anyone who believes in it as God's word." That sounds dangerous. . . .*[9]

At this point we must answer that indeed it does.

The second common characteristic of higher criticism is its *naturalism,* expressed in the belief that *the Bible is the result of an evolutionary process.* Evidence of this belief can be seen in Old Testament studies in the way the documentary theory of the Pentateuch developed. The belief is also evident in Bultmann's form criticism, for everything depends on the early church's gradually developing its understanding of reality and preserving it at various stages through the written traditions. Early and primitive understandings of God and reality are presumed to have given way to later, more developed conceptions. So-called primitive ideas may be rejected in favor of more modern ones. Thus, reports of miracles may be discounted. Also, according to this view, crude notions such as the wrath of God, sacrifice and a visible Second Coming of the Lord may be excluded from the religion of the New Testament.

The third major characteristic of the higher criticism is based on the first two. If people and their ideas change as the evolutionary hypothesis speculates, then they will continue to change; they have changed since the last books of the Bible were written; consequently, _we must go beyond the Scriptures to understand both humanity and true religion._ There are many examples of this attitude, particularly in popular sermons in which the viewpoints of secular thinkers are often widely aired while the contrary views of the biblical writers are forgotten.

A Reply

What is to be said in reply to this widespread and popular approach? There are two perspectives. On the one hand, there is a neutral area in which anyone may properly use at least some parts of the critical method. It may be used to illuminate the human element in the biblical writings. Attention may be given to words and their varying uses, the historical situation out of which the writings came and the unique features of the various biblical books. Besides, there are matters of archaeology and parallel secular history, both of which shed light on the texts. Use of the method in these areas and in this way is valuable. On the other hand the best-known exponents of the critical method have proceeded on assumptions unacceptable to true biblical theologians, and the method may therefore be judged a failure in their hands.

First, users of the critical method demand the right to be scientific in their examination of the biblical data. But they are vulnerable, not when they are scientific but rather when *they fail to be scientific enough.* The negative literary critics presuppose the right to examine the Bible in a manner identical to that which they would use in studying any secular literature. But is it valid to approach Scripture as nothing more than a collection of secular writings? Is it scientific or wise to neglect the fact that the books claim to be the result of the "breathing-out" of God? Can a decision on this matter really be postponed while an examination of the books goes forward? If the books really are from God, doesn't their nature in itself limit the critical options?

It is futile as well as erroneous to deny the critics the right to examine the biblical texts. They will do it whether they are asked to or not. Besides, if the Scriptures are truth, they must stand up beneath the barrage of any valid critical method; we must not make the mistake of the fundamentalists of the nineteenth century in claiming a special exemption for the Bible. On the other hand, it must be maintained that any critical method must also take into consideration the nature of the material at its disposal. In the case of the Bible, criticism must either accept its claims to be the Word of God or else offer satisfactory reasons for rejecting them. If the Bible is the Word of God, as it claims to be, then criticism must include an understanding of revelation in its methodological procedure.

The failure of criticism to do this is nowhere more apparent than in its efforts to divorce the Jesus of history from the Christ of faith. If Jesus were no more than a human being and the Bible no more than a human book, this could be done. But if Christ is divine and if the Bible is the Word of the Father about him, then it is the obligation of criticism to recognize the nature of the Gospels as a divine and binding interpretation of the life, death and resurrection of Jesus of Nazareth, the Son of God. With a firm appreciation of the Bible as revelation, literary criticism would be free, on the one hand, from all charges of irreverence and abuse and, on the other, from an easy and unfounded optimism that would place the solution to all biblical problems within easy grasp.

The same failure is evident in the critics' treatment of the Bible as the result of a human evolutionary process, according to which one part of Scripture may easily contradict another. If the Bible is really from God, these will not be contradictions but rather complementary or progressive disclosures of one truth.

Second, having failed to accept the Bible for what it truly is, negative critics inevitably fall into error as they proceed on other premises. Thus, they eventually display *their own inherent weaknesses*. One clear example of this is the old quest for the historical Jesus which, as was pointed out earlier, simply molded the historical Christ into the interpreter's own image. Another example is Bultmann who, although he once enjoyed almost legendary renown, is today increasingly deserted by his followers.

They ask: If, as Bultmann says, virtually all we need to know of the historicity of the Christian faith is the mere "thatness" of Jesus Christ, his existence, then why even that? Why was the Incarnation necessary? And if it was *not* really necessary or if it is impossible to show *why* it was necessary, what is to keep the Christian faith from degenerating into the realm of abstract ideas? And what in that case is to distinguish its view of the Incarnation from Docetism or from a Gnostic redeemer-myth?

Ernst Kaesemann of Marburg, Bultmann's old stomping ground, raised these questions in a now famous address to the reunion of old Marburg students in 1953. He argued, "We cannot do away with the identity between the exalted and the earthly Lord without falling into Docetism and depriving ourselves of the possibility of drawing a line between the Easter faith of the community and myth."[10] A few years later Joachim Jeremias voiced a similar warning. "We are in danger

of surrendering the affirmation 'the Word became flesh' and
of abandoning the salvation-history, God's activity in the Man
Jesus of Nàzareth and in His message; we are in danger of
approaching Docetism, where Christ becomes an idea."[11]

Even Bultmann's supporters must find it a bit incongruous
that his *Theology of the New Testament* gives only thirty pages to
the teachings of Jesus while devoting more than one hundred
pages to an imaginary account of the theology of the so-called
Hellenistic communities, of which we know nothing.

Bultmann has minimized both the early church's concern
for the facts of Jesus' life and its dependence upon him as
teacher. While it is true, as Bultmann argues, that the biblical
documents are concerned primarily with Jesus' identity as the
Messiah and with the revelation he brings of the Father, it is
no less significant that their understanding of him is em-
bodied, not in theological tracts or cosmic mythologies (as in
Gnosticism), but in Gospels. Their structure is historical.
Moreover, every verse of the Gospels seems to cry out that
the origin of the Christian faith lies, not in the sudden enlightenment of the early Christians or in an evolving religious
experience, but in the facts concerning Jesus Christ: his life,
death and particularly his resurrection. Even the kerygma
proclaims the historical event, for it was Jesus of Nazareth
who died for our sins according to the Scriptures, was buried
and who rose again on the third day, according to the Scriptures (1 Cor. 15:3-4).[12]

A third objection to this type of higher criticism is the most
important one. Such critics have *a very small god.* They don't
deny the existence of God entirely, but they do minimize his
ability and his presence. He can speak to the individual, but he
cannot guarantee the content of that revelation or preserve
it in a reliable, written form. He can act in history, but he cannot act miraculously. Can miracles occur? If they can, then
much of what the higher critics dismiss as mythological has a
very good claim to being historical. If they can, the God of

miracles is capable of giving us an authoritative and infallible revelation.

For all its alleged objectivity, in the ultimate analysis modern criticism is unable to escape the great questions: Is there a God? Is the God of the Bible the true God? Has God revealed himself in the Bible and in Jesus of Nazareth as the focal point of the written revelation? If, as has been suggested, it is necessary for criticism to deal with the full nature of the material, in particular with the claims of the Bible to be the Word of God as well as words written by particular people, then it must deal with a question that involves either denial or the response of faith.

When criticism faces the fact that the portrait of Jesus appearing in the Gospels makes the humble man from Nazareth the Son of God, then it must ask whether or not this interpretation is the right one, and if so, it must accept his teachings. When it confronts the Bible's claims regarding its own nature, it must ask and answer whether the Bible is indeed God's express revelation. If the answers to these questions are Yes, then a new kind of criticism will emerge. This new criticism will treat the biblical statements as being true rather than errant, it will look for complementary statements rather than contradictions, and it will perceive the voice of God (as well as the voices of people) throughout. Such a criticism will be judged by the Scriptures rather than the other way around.

8 HOW TO INTERPRET THE BIBLE

"Some books are to be tasted, others to be swallowed, and some few to be chewed and digested; that is, some are to be read only in parts; others to be read, but not curiously; and some few to be read wholly, and with diligence and attention."[1]

The seventeenth-century English essayist Sir Francis Bacon was not thinking exclusively of the Bible as he wrote these words. But there is little doubt that if the admonition "to be read wholly and with diligence and attention" is to be applied to any book, it is certainly to be applied to the Scriptures of the Old and New Testaments which are the Word of God. The Bible is one form of God's gracious revelation of himself to men and women. It should be highly cherished. Love for God plus a desire to know him better as well as to obey his express commands should compel us to study it diligently.

But here a problem develops. If the Bible is God's book, given to us over a period of approximately fifteen hundred years by more than forty human authors, obviously it is unlike any other book we have encountered. The principles of study would therefore seem to be different. Are they? If so, what should they be? Should the Bible be considered spiritually—that is, in a mystical or magical sense? Those who take that approach seem to be led into strange and irrational persuasions. Or should it be read in a purely natural manner—that is, as we would read any other book? The latter course seems proper, but this is the avowed purpose of the naturalistic higher criticism, which we have criticized strongly. What should the approach of the Christian reader or the Christian scholar be?

The answers are found in the four most important truths about the Bible, all of which have been covered in the previous chapters: (1) the Bible has one true author, who is God; (2) the Bible is given to us through human channels; (3) the Bible has a unifying purpose, namely, to lead us to an obedient and worshipful knowledge of the true God; and (4) understanding the Bible requires the supernatural activity of the Holy Spirit whose work it is to interpret the Scriptures to us. The essential principles for study of God's Word are implied in these four propositions.

One Book, One Author, One Theme

First, the Scriptures have but one author and that is God. True, the Bible has also come by means of human channels, but far more important is the fact that the Bible as a whole and in all its parts is from God. Superficially, a person may see the Bible as a miscellaneous collection of writings tied together more or less by the accidents of history. But the Bible isn't just a collection. It is, as J. I. Packer states, "a single book with a single author—God the Spirit—and a single theme—God the Son, and the Father's saving purposes, which all revolve around him."[2]

The Bible's authorship leads to two principles of interpretation: the principle of *unity* and the principle of *noncontradic-*

tion. Taken together they mean that, if the Bible is truly from God and if God is a God of truth (as he is), then (1) the parts of the book must go together to tell one story, and (2) if two parts seem to be in opposition or in contradiction to each other, our interpretation of one or both of these parts must be in error. It might even be said that if a scholar is expending his efforts to highlight contradictions in the biblical text and is not going beyond that to indicate how they may be resolved, he is not demonstrating his wisdom or honesty so much as he is demonstrating his failure as an interpreter of the Word of God.

Many will claim that an attempt to find unity where they say there is none is dishonesty. But the problem is actually one of interpretation and presuppositions.

We may take the matter of sacrifices as an example. Everyone recognizes that sacrifices play a large role in the Old Testament, and that they are not emphasized in the New Testament. Why is this? How are we to regard them? Here one person brings in his idea of an evolving religious conscience. He supposes that sacrifices are important in the most primitive forms of religion. They are to be explained by the individual's fear of the gods or God. God is imagined to be a capricious, vengeful deity, so worshipers try to appease him by sacrifice. This seems to be the general idea of sacrifice in the pagan religions of antiquity. It is assumed for the religion of the ancient Semite peoples too.

In time, however, such a primitive view of God is imagined to give way to a more elevated conception of him. God is then seen not so much as a God of capricious whim and wrath, but rather a God of justice. So law begins to take a more prominent place, eventually replacing sacrifice as the center of the religion. Finally, the worshipers rise to the conception of God as a God of love, and at that point sacrifice disappears entirely. The one who thinks this way might fix the turning point at the coming of Jesus Christ and his teachings. Therefore, today he would disregard both sacrifices and the idea of the wrath of God as outmoded concepts.

By contrast, another person (an evangelical might fall in this category) would approach the material with entirely different presuppositions and would therefore produce an entirely different interpretation. He or she would begin by noting that the Old Testament does indeed tell a great deal about the wrath of God. But he would note that this element is hardly eliminated as one goes on through the Bible, most certainly not through the New Testament. It is, for instance, one of Paul's important themes. It emerges strongly in the book of Revelation where we read about God's just wrath eventually being poured out against the sins of a rebellious and ungodly race. As far as sacrifices are concerned, it is true that the detailed sacrifices of the Old Testament system are no longer performed in the New Testament churches. But their disappearance is not because a supposed primitive conception of God has given way to a more advanced one but rather because the great sacrifice of Jesus Christ has completed and superseded them all, as the book of Hebrews clearly maintains.

For such a person the solution is not to be found in an evolving conception of God; for him, God is always the same—a God of wrath toward sin, a God of love toward the sinner. Rather it is to be found in God's progressive revelation of himself to mankind, a revelation in which the sacrifices (for which God gives explicit instructions) are intended to teach both the serious nature of sin and the way in which God had always determined to save sinners. The Old Testament sacrifices point to Christ. John the Baptist is able to say, referring to part of the sacrificial system in ancient Jewish life that all would understand, "Behold, the Lamb of God, who takes away the sin of the world!" (Jn. 1:29). And Peter can write, "You know that you were ransomed from the futile ways inherited from your fathers, not with perishable things such as silver or gold, but with the precious blood of Christ, like that of a lamb without blemish or spot" (1 Pet. 1:18-19).

In this example, as in all cases of biblical interpretation, the data are the same. The only difference is that one approaches Scripture looking for contradiction and development. The other approaches Scripture as if God has written it and therefore looks for unity, allowing one passage to throw light on another. The Westminster Confession states: "The infallible rule of interpretation of Scripture is the Scripture itself: and therefore, when there is a question about the true and full sense of any Scripture (which is not manifold, but one), it must be searched and known by other places that speak more clearly" (I, ix).

Human Channels

A second truth about the Bible is that it has been given to us through human channels even though God is the ultimate source of the Scriptures. Its human component does not mean that the Bible is therefore subject to error as all merely human books are. But it does mean that all sound principles of interpretation must be used in studying the Bible, precisely as they would be used in the study of any other ancient document. The way into the mind of God is through the mind of the human author, whom he used as a channel. Consequently, the only proper way to interpret the Bible is to discover what God's human speakers were concerned to express.

One necessary part of interpretation is to consider each biblical statement in *context;* that is, within the context of the chapter, the book and eventually the entire Word of God. Understanding the context is an obvious need in the interpretation of any document. Taking a statement out of context is almost always misleading. But it is to be guarded against in interpreting the Bible especially, since Bible-believing people have such regard for the words of Scripture that they sometimes elevate them at the expense of the context. Frank E. Gaebelein, author of a valuable book on interpreting the Bible, says,

Realizing that the Bible is God's inspired Word, the devout reader attaches peculiar importance to every statement it contains. This reverence is commendable, but when it descends to the practice of picking out single verses as proofs of all sorts of things, it becomes positively dangerous. Were this a sound method of interpretation, one could find biblical support for nearly all the crimes on the calendar, from drunkenness and murder to lying and deceit. [3]

The Bible itself speaks of the need for proper interpretation: "Do your best to present yourself to God as one approved, a workman who has no need to be ashamed, rightly handling the word of truth" (2 Tim. 2:15). In this verse, the word translated "rightly handling" literally means "to cut straight" or "handle correctly."

A second need is to consider the *style* of the material and then to interpret it within that framework. Consideration of style is obviously important in dealing with poetical literature such as the book of Psalms, Proverbs, Job and even parts of prophetic material. The poetic books frequently employ symbols or images; they are misinterpreted if metaphors are taken literally. The book of Revelation is not to be taken literally in all its parts, as, for example, the vision of Jesus found in the opening verses. The result of a literal interpretation is a monstrosity, giving us a figure who is entirely white, having hair like wool, eyes like fire, feet like heated and glowing bronze, a sword going out of his mouth, with seven stars in his right hand. On the other hand, when each of these items is discovered to be an image associated with God in the Old Testament, then the vision yields us a portrait of Jesus who is thereby shown to be one with God the Father in all his attributes: holy, eternal, omniscient, omnipresent, revealing and sovereign.

The matter of style also has its bearing upon the New Testament parables. The use of parables was a special method of teaching and must be recognized as such. Usually a parable makes one or, at best, a few main points. Consequently it is an error to fix an application to each detail of the story. For example, an attempt to assign a meaning to the husks, pigs and other details of the story of the prodigal son is ludicrous.

A third need is to consider the *purpose* for which a particular passage was written. In other words, we must consider its scope. Gaebelein writes,

The Bible has a single great purpose. It was given to reveal the love of God as manifested in the divine provision of salvation through our Lord Jesus Christ. This is its aim, and sound interpretation must never lose sight of this aim. Consequently, it is a serious and misleading error to regard the Bible as a source-book on science, philosophy, or any subject other than its central theme of the Deity in relation to humanity. After all, there is a proper scope of Scripture, a scope determined not by individual writers, inspired though they were, but by the divine Author of it all. One cannot hold the Bible accountable for fields of knowledge outside the scope delineated by the divine purpose of the book. [4]*

One obvious application is to those references that seem to have bothered Rudolf Bultmann so much, in which heaven is assumed to be "up there" and hell "below" our feet. Again, a consideration of purpose or scope applies to passages about bones crying out, bowels yearning, kidneys instructing and ears judging. It is often said that such references reveal a mistaken notion of the universe and of human physiology, but this is absurd. All they show is that the biblical writers wrote in the language of their day, so that they would be understood. Their use of such phrases is no more scientific than our use of phrases like "walking on air," a "gut feeling," "deep in my heart" and so on.

It is not always easy to determine whether a passage is using literal or figurative language, of course, so we must be careful. Most important is to be aware of the problem and consciously to seek for the true scope of the passage. In seeking its purpose we may ask such questions as: To whom is it written? Who has written it? When was it written? What does it say?

A fourth need is to give full attention to the *meaning of the individual words.* It is possible that God can think without words or other symbols, but it is certain that we cannot. Consequently, the meaning of words and an individual's use of them are of great importance. When we fail to take them into consideration, we inevitably misinterpret.

Obviously Bible students must not fail to give close attention to the precise meaning of the biblical words. Word studies themselves can be extremely rewarding; words like "faith," "salvation," "righteousness," "love," "spirit," "glory," "church," and many others are fascinating.

The summary of these points is contained in what has come to be called the historical-literal method of biblical interpretation. The method simply means, as Packer puts it, that "the proper, natural sense of each passage (i.e., the intended sense of the writer) is to be taken as fundamental." The intended meaning of the words in their own context and in the speech of the original writer or spokesman is the starting point.

> *In other words, Scripture statements must be interpreted in the light of the rules of grammar and discourse on the one hand, and of their own place in history on the other. This is what we should expect in the nature of the case, seeing that the biblical books originated as occasional documents addressed to contemporary audiences; and it is exemplified in the New Testament exposition of the Old, from which the fanciful allegorizing practised by Philo and the Rabbis is strikingly absent.*[5]

The principle is based on the fact that the Bible is God's Word in human language. It means that Scripture is to be interpreted in its natural sense, and that theological or cultural preferences must not be allowed to obscure the fundamental meaning.

Responding to the Word

Third, the Bible is given by God in order to provoke a personal response in us. If we don't allow that to happen, we in-

evitably misuse the Bible (even in studying it) and misinterpret it. Once Christ told the Jewish leaders of his day, "You
search the scriptures, because you think that in them you have
eternal life; and it is they that bear witness to me; yet you refuse to come to me that you may have life. I do not receive
glory from men. But I know that you have not the love of God
within you.... How can you believe, who receive glory from
one another and do not seek the glory that comes from the
only God?" (Jn. 5:39-42, 44).

No one could charge the Jews of Christ's day with having a
low opinion of the Scriptures, for they actually had the highest regard for them. Nor could they be faulted for a lack of
meticulous study. The Jews did study the Scriptures. They
prized them. Yet in their high regard for the Bible they passed
over its intention: their lives were not changed. Although they
gained human acclaim for their detailed knowledge of the
Bible, they did not gain salvation.

In John's Gospel we are told of the healing of a man who
had been born blind. The meat of the story lies in the fact that,
like everyone, he was also spiritually blind before Christ
touched him. Afterward he came to spiritual sight.

When the man was healed, he came into conflict with the
Jewish rulers. They knew about Jesus, but they didn't believe
in him. In fact, they didn't believe in him precisely because of
their attitude to the Scriptures. For them the revelation recorded in the Old Testament was an end in itself. Nothing
could be added and nothing was required. They said, "We
know that God has spoken to Moses, but as for this man, we do
not know where he comes from" (Jn. 9:29). The man who had
been born blind didn't try to compete with them in their mas-
tery of the Old Testament, but he pointed to the unquestion-
able fact of his healing. He concluded, "If this man were not
from God, he could do nothing" (v. 33). In treating the Old
Testament as an end in itself, the Jews, therefore, actually
perverted it and missed its true meaning. They failed to see

that it is precisely to Jesus that the Old Testament law (which came through Moses) testified.

The same thing happens when a person buys a beautiful Bible to place in an important position in his or her home but doesn't read it. Why do people do such a thing? In their minds the Bible is something special. They have a reverence for it. But their belief does not go beyond superstition. As a result, they never read it and never come into contact with its Author.

This is one error of those of Christ's day. But that wasn't their only error. They also became so preoccupied with the details of Scripture that they missed the truths contained there. For instance, the scribes, whose work it was to copy the Scriptures, subjected the pages of the Bible to the closest scrutiny. They gave attention to every syllable. They even counted the words and letters so that they knew which of them came in the middle of the page and how many of each a given page should have. We can be thankful for their meticulous care, for the accuracy of our present Old Testament texts is the result of it. Nevertheless, in many cases the interaction of the copier with the Word of God stopped with the copying.

Many people today have a high degree of biblical knowledge. They can name the twelve apostles, the cities Paul visited, the list of Hebrew kings and so on. But they have missed what the Scriptures have to teach about sin, justification, the Christian life and obedience. Many others make a mistake in being preoccupied with prophecy.

Jesus said that we will know the truth about himself only if we are willing to do his will, that is, if we allow ourselves to be changed by the truths we find in Scripture. He said, "If any man's will is to do his will [that is, if he determines to do it], he shall know whether the teaching is from God or whether I am speaking on my own authority" (Jn. 7:17). We must not assume that we will be able fully to understand any passage of Scripture unless we are willing to be changed by it.

Taught by the Spirit

A final point lies in the internal witness of the Spirit to the truth of the Word of God. Here Scripture speaks succinctly. Not only was the Holy Spirit active in the writing of the biblical books, he is also active in conveying the truth of the Bible to the minds of those who read it. Paul writes, "We have received not the spirit of the world, but the Spirit which is from God, that we might understand the gifts bestowed on us by God. And we impart this in words not taught by human wisdom but taught by the Spirit, interpreting spiritual truths to those who possess the Spirit" (1 Cor. 2:12-13). The Bible deals with spiritual themes, and therefore it requires the activity of the Holy Spirit for us to understand them. The Holy Spirit is the teacher of Christians. It is he who brings forth new life in those who hear the gospel.

So we must pray as we study the Scriptures, and we must ask the Holy Spirit to do his work of enlightenment in our hearts. The Spirit's presence is not given to us to make a careful and diligent study of the Word of God unnecessary. He is given to make our study effective.

God speaks in the Bible. We must allow him to speak, and we must listen to what he will say to us. One day at the height of the Reformation Martin Luther was asked to autograph the flyleaf of a Bible, as often happened after his own translation was published. He took the Bible and wrote down John 8:25. "Who are you? . . . Even what I have told you from the beginning." Then Luther added,

> They . . . desire to know who he is and not to regard what he says, while he desires them first to listen; then they will know who he is. The rule is: Listen and allow the Word to make the beginning; then the knowing will nicely follow. If, however, you do not listen, then you will never know anything. For it is decreed: God will not be seen, known, or comprehended except through his Word alone. Whatever, therefore, one undertakes for salvation apart from the Word is in vain. God will not respond to that. He will not have it.

He will not tolerate it any other way. Therefore, let his Book, in which he speaks with you, be commended to you; for he did not cause it to be written for no purpose. He did not want us to let it lie there in neglect, as if he were speaking with mice under the bench or with flies on the pulpit. We are to read it, to think and speak about it, and to study it, certain that he himself (not an angel or a creature) is speaking with us in it.[6]

The one who reads the Bible prayerfully, thoughtfully and receptively will discover that it is indeed the Word of God and that it is "profitable for teaching, for reproof, for correction, and for training in righteousness, that the man of God may be complete, equipped for every good work" (2 Tim. 3:16-17).

PART III
THE ATTRIBUTES OF GOD

God said to Moses, "I AM WHO I AM." And he said, "Say this to the people of Israel, 'I AM has sent me to you.'" (Ex. 3:14)

"Go therefore and make disciples of all nations, baptizing them in the name of the Father and of the Son and of the Holy Spirit." (Mt. 28:19)

Thine, O LORD, is the greatness, and the power, and the glory, and the victory, and the majesty; for all that is in the heavens and in the earth is thine; thine is the kingdom, O LORD, and thou art exalted as head above all. (1 Chron. 29:11)

And the four living creatures, each of them with six wings, are full of eyes all round and within, and day and night they never cease to sing, "Holy, holy, holy, is the Lord God Almighty, who was and is and is to come!" (Rev. 4:8)

O the depth of the riches and wisdom and knowledge of God! How unsearchable are his judgments and how inscrutable his ways! "For who has known the mind of the Lord, or who has been his counselor?" (Rom. 11:33-34)

"I the LORD do not change." (Mal. 3:6)

9

THE
TRUE
GOD

It is evident that we need more than a theoretical knowledge of God. Yet we can know God only as he reveals himself to us in the Scriptures, and we cannot know the Scriptures until we are willing to be changed by them. Knowledge of God occurs only when we also know our deep spiritual need and when we are receptive to God's gracious provision for our need through the work of Christ and the application of that work to us by God's Spirit.

Having established this base, we nevertheless come back to the question of God himself and we ask, "But who is God? Who is this one who reveals himself in Scripture, in the person of Jesus Christ and through the Holy Spirit?" We may admit that a true knowledge of God must change us. We may be willing to be changed. But where do we begin?

"I Am Who I Am"
Since the Bible is a unity we could answer these questions by starting at any point in the biblical revelation. We could begin

with Revelation 22:21 as well as with Genesis 1:1. But there is no better starting point than God's revelation of himself to Moses at the burning bush. Moses, the great leader of Israel, had long been aware of the true God, for he had been born into a godly family. Still, when God said that he would send him to Egypt and through him deliver the people of Israel, Moses responded, "If I come to the people of Israel and say to them, 'The God of your fathers has sent me to you,' and they ask me, 'What is his name?' what shall I say to them?" We are told that God then answered Moses by saying, "I AM WHO I AM.... Say this to the people of Israel, 'I AM has sent me to you' " (Ex. 3:13-14).

"I AM WHO I AM." The name is linked with the ancient name for God, Jehovah. But it is more than a name. It is a descriptive name, pointing to all that God is in himself. In particular, it shows him to be the One who is entirely self-existent, self-sufficient and eternal.

These are abstract concepts, of course. But they are important, for these attributes more than any others set God apart from his creation and reveal him as being what he is in himself. God is perfect in all his attributes. But there are some attributes that we, his creatures, share. For instance, God is perfect in his love. Yet by his grace we also love. He is all wise; but we also possess a measure of wisdom. He is all powerful; and we exercise a limited power. It is not like that in regard to God's self-existence, self-sufficiency and eternity, however. He alone possesses those characteristics. He exists in and of himself; we do not. He is entirely self-sufficient; we are not. He is eternal; we are newcomers on the scene.

Self-existence means that God has no origins and consequently is answerable to no one. Matthew Henry says, "The greatest and best man in the world must say, By the grace of God *I am what I am;* but God says absolutely—and it is more than any creature, man or angel, can say—*I am that I am.*"[1] So God has no origins; his existence does not depend on anybody.

Self-existence is a hard concept for us to grapple with for it means that God as he is in himself is _unknowable._ Everything that we see, smell, hear, taste or touch has origins. We can hardly think in any other category. Anything we observe must have a cause adequate to explain it. We seek for such causes. Cause and effect is even the basis for the belief in God possessed by those who, nevertheless, don't truly know him. Such individuals believe in God, not because they have had a personal experience of him or because they have discovered God in Scripture, but only because they infer his existence. "Everything comes from something; consequently, there must be a great something that stands behind everything." Cause and effect point to God, but—and this is the issue—they point to a God who is beyond understanding, indeed to one who is beyond us in every way. They indicate that God cannot be known and evaluated like other things can.

A. W. Tozer has noted that this is one reason why philosophy and science have not always been friendly toward the idea of God. These disciplines are dedicated to the task of accounting for things as we know them and are therefore impatient with anything that refuses to give an account of itself. Philosophers and scientists will admit that there is much they don't know. But it is another thing to admit that there is something they can never know completely and which, in fact, they don't even have techniques for discovering. To discover God, scientists may attempt to bring God down to their level, defining him as "natural law," "evolution" or some such principle. But still God eludes them. There is more to God than any such concepts can delineate.

Perhaps, too, this is why even Bible-believing people seem to spend so little time thinking about God's person and character. Tozer writes,

> _Few of us have let our hearts gaze in wonder at the I AM, the self-existent Self back of which no creature can think. Such thoughts are too painful for us. We prefer to think where it will do more_

good—about how to build a better mousetrap, for instance, or how to make two blades of grass grow where one grew before. And for this we are now paying a too heavy price in the secularization of our religion and the decay of our inner lives. [2]

God's self-existence means that *he is not answerable* to us or to anybody, and we don't like that. We want God to give an account of himself, to defend his actions. Although he sometimes explains things to us, he doesn't have to and often he does not. God doesn't have to explain himself to anybody.

No Needs

The second quality of God communicated to us in the name "I AM WHO I AM" is self-sufficiency. Again it is possible to have at least a sense of the meaning of this abstract term. Self-sufficiency means God has no needs and therefore depends on no one.

Here we run counter to a widespread and popular idea: God cooperates with human beings, each thereby supplying something lacking in the other. It is imagined, for example, that God lacks glory and therefore creates men and women to supply it. He takes care of them as a reward. Or again, it is imagined that God needs love and therefore creates men and women to love him. Some talk about the creation as if God were lonely and therefore created us to keep him company. On a practical level we see the same thing in those who imagine that women and men are necessary to carry out God's work of salvation as witnesses or as defenders of the faith, forgetting that Jesus himself declared that "God is able from these stones to raise up children to Abraham" (Lk. 3:8).

God does not need *worshipers.* Arthur W. Pink, who writes on this theme in *The Attributes of God,* says,

God was under no constraint, no obligation, no necessity to create. That he chose to do so was purely a sovereign act on his part, caused by nothing outside himself, determined by nothing but his own mere good pleasure; for he "worketh all things after the counsel of his

_own will" (Eph. 1:11). That he did create was simply for his
manifestative glory. . . . God is no gainer even from our worship.
He was in no need of that external glory of his grace which arises
from his redeemed, for he is glorious enough in himself without that.
What was it moved him to predestinate his elect to the praise of the
glory of his grace? It was, as Ephesians 1:5 tells us, "according to
the good pleasure of his will." . . . The force of this is [that] it is
impossible to bring the Almighty under obligations to the creature;
God gains nothing from us._ [3]

Tozer makes the same point. "Were all human beings suddenly to become blind, still the sun would shine by day and the
stars by night, for these owe nothing to the millions who benefit from their light. So, were every man on earth to become
atheist, it could not affect God in any way. He is what he is in
himself without regard to any other. To believe in him adds
nothing to his perfections; to doubt him takes nothing away." [4]

Nor does God need _helpers_. This truth is probably harder
for us to accept than almost any other. For we imagine God as
a friendly, but almost pathetic, grandfather figure bustling
about to see whom he can find to help him in managing the
world and saving the world's race. What a travesty! To be sure,
God has entrusted a work of management to us. He said to the
original pair in Eden, "Be fruitful and multiply, and fill the
earth and subdue it; and have dominion over the fish of the
sea and over the birds of the air and over every living thing
that moves upon the earth" (Gen. 1:28). God also has given
those who believe in him a commission to "go into all the world
and preach the gospel to the whole creation" (Mk. 16:15).
True, but no aspect of God's ordering of his creation has a
necessary grounding in himself. God has chosen to do things
thus. He didn't need to do them. Indeed, he could have done
them in any one of a million other ways. That he did choose to
do things thus is therefore solely dependent upon the free
and sovereign exercise of his will and so does not give us any
inherent value to him.

To say that God is self-sufficient also means that God does not need *defenders.* Clearly, we have opportunities to speak for God before those who would dishonor his name and malign his character. We ought to do so. But even if we should fail, we must not think that God is deprived thereby. God does not need to be defended, for he is as he is and will remain so regardless of the sinful and arrogant attacks of evil individuals. A God who needs to be defended is no God. Rather, the God of the Bible is the self-existent One who is the true defender of his people.

When we realize that God is the only truly self-sufficient One, we begin to understand why the Bible has so much to say about the need for faith in God alone and why unbelief in God is such sin. Tozer writes: "Among all created beings, not one dare trust in itself. God alone trusts in himself; all other beings must trust in him. Unbelief is actually perverted faith, for it puts its trust not in the living God but in dying men."[5] If we refuse to trust God, what we are actually saying is that either we or some other person or thing is more trustworthy. That is a slander against the character of God, and it is folly. Nothing else is all-sufficient. On the other hand, if we begin by trusting God (by believing in him), we have a solid foundation for all life. God is sufficient, and his Word to his creatures can be trusted.

Because God is sufficient, we may begin by resting in that sufficiency and so work effectively for him. God does not need us. But the joy of coming to know him is in learning that he nevertheless stoops to work in and through those who are his believing and obedient children.

Alpha and Omega

A third quality inherent in the name of God given to Moses ("I AM WHO I AM") is everlastingness, perpetuity or eternity. The quality is difficult to put in one word, but it is simply that God is, has always been and will always be, and that he is ever the same in his eternal being. We find this attribute of God everywhere in the Bible. Abraham called Jehovah "the Everlasting God" (Gen. 21:33). Moses wrote, "LORD, thou hast been our dwelling place in all generations. Before the mountains were brought forth, or ever thou hadst formed the earth and the world, from everlasting to everlasting thou art God" (Ps. 90:1-2). The book of Revelation describes God as the "Alpha and the Omega, the beginning and the end" (Rev. 1:8; 21:6; 22:13). The creatures before the throne cry, "Holy, holy, holy, is the Lord God Almighty, who was and is and is to come" (Rev. 4:8).

The fact that God is eternal has two major consequences for us. The first is that *he can be trusted* to remain as he reveals himself to be. The word usually used to describe this quality is immutability, which means unchangeableness. "Every good endowment and every perfect gift is from above, coming down from the Father of lights with whom there is no variation or shadow due to change" (Jas. 1:17).

God is unchangeable in his attributes. So we need not fear, for example, that the God who once loved us in Christ will somehow change his mind and cease to love us in the future. God is always love toward his people. Similarly, we must not think that perhaps he will change his attitude toward sin, so that he will begin to classify as "permissible" something that was formerly prohibited. Sin will always be sin because it is defined as any transgression of or lack of conformity to the law of God, who is unchangeable. God will always be holy, wise, gracious, just and everything else that he reveals himself to be. Nothing that we do will ever change the eternal God.

God is also unchangeable in his counsels or will. He does what he has determined beforehand to do and his will never varies. Some will point out that certain verses in the Bible tell us that God repented of some act—as in Genesis 6:6, "The LORD was sorry that he had made man." In this example, a human word is being used to indicate God's severe displeasure with human activities. It is countered by such verses as Numbers 23:19 ("God is not man, that he should lie, or a son of man, that he should repent. Has he said, and will he not do it? Or has he spoken, and will he not fulfil it?"); 1 Samuel 15:29 ("The Glory of Israel will not lie or repent; for he is not a man, that he should repent"); Romans 11:29 ("The gifts and call of God are irrevocable"); and Psalm 33:11 ("The counsel of the LORD stands for ever, the thoughts of his heart to all generations").

Such statements are a source of great comfort to God's people. If God were like us, he could not be relied on. He would change, and as a result of that his will and his promises would change. We could not depend on him. But God is not like us. He does not change. Consequently, his purposes remain fixed from generation to generation. Pink says, "Here then is a rock on which we may fix our feet, while the mighty torrent is sweeping away everything around us. The permanence of God's character guarantees the fulfillment of his promises."[6]

The second major consequence for us of God's unchangeableness is that he is *inescapable.* If he were a mere human and if we didn't like either him or what he was doing, we might ignore him knowing that he might always change his mind, move away from us or die. But God does not change his mind. He does not move away. He will not die. Consequently, we cannot escape him. Even if we ignore him now, we must reckon with him in the life to come. If we reject him now, we must eventually face the One we have rejected and come to know his eternal rejection of us.

No Other Gods

We are led to a natural conclusion, namely, that we should seek and worship the true God. This chapter has been based for the most part on Exodus 3:14, in which God reveals to Moses the name by which he desires to be known. That revelation came on the verge of the deliverance of the people of Israel from Egypt. After the exodus, God gave a revelation on Mount Sinai which applies the earlier disclosure of himself as the true God to the religious life and worship of the delivered nation.

God said, "I am the LORD your God, who brought you out of the land of Egypt, out of the house of bondage. You shall have no other gods before me. You shall not make for yourself a graven image, or any likeness of anything that is in heaven above, or that is in the earth beneath, or that is in the water under the earth; you shall not bow down to them or serve them; for I the LORD your God am a jealous God, visiting the iniquity of the fathers upon the children to the third and the fourth generation of those who hate me, but showing steadfast love to thousands of those who love me and keep my commandments" (Ex. 20:2-6). These verses make three points, all based on the premise that the God who reveals himself in the Bible is the true God:

1. We are to worship God and obey him.
2. We are to reject the worship of any other god.
3. We are to reject the worship of the true God by any means that are unworthy of him, such as the use of pictures or images.

At first glance it seems quite strange that a prohibition against the use of images in worship should have a place at the very start of the ten basic principles of biblical religion, the Ten Commandments. But it is not strange when we remember that the characteristics of a religion flow from the nature of the religion's god. If the god is unworthy, the religion will be unworthy too. If the concept of God is of the highest order, the religion will be of a high order also. So God tells us in these verses that any physical representation of him is dishonoring to him. Why? For two reasons. First, it obscures his glory, for nothing visible can ever adequately represent it. Second, it misleads those who would worship him.

Both of these errors are represented by Aaron's manufacture of the golden calf, as J. I. Packer indicates in his discussion of idolatry. In Aaron's mind, at least, though probably not in the minds of the people, the calf was intended to represent Jehovah. He thought, no doubt, that a figure of a bull (even a small one) communicated the thought of God's strength. But, of course, it didn't do so adequately. And it didn't at all communicate his other great attributes: his sovereignty, righteousness, mercy, love and justice. Rather, it obscured them.

Moreover, the figure of the bull misled the worshipers. They readily associated it with the fertility gods and goddesses of Egypt, and the result of their worship was an orgy. Packer concludes,

It is certain that if you habitually focus your thoughts on an image or picture of the One to whom you are going to pray, you will come to think of him, and pray to him, as the image represents him. Thus you will in this sense "bow down" and "worship" your image; and to the extent to which the image fails to tell the truth about God, to that extent you will fail to worship God in truth. That is why God forbids you and me to make use of images and pictures in our worship. [7]

"My Lord and My God"

To avoid the worship of images or even the use of images in the worship of the true God is not in itself worship. We are to recognize that the true God is the eternal, self-existent and self-sufficient One, the One immeasurably beyond our highest thoughts. Therefore, we are to humble ourselves and learn from him, allowing him to teach us what he is like and what he has done for our salvation. Do we do what he commands? Are we sure that in our worship we are actually worshiping the true God who has revealed himself in the Bible?

There is only one way to answer that question truthfully. It is to ask: Do I really know the Bible, and do I worship God on the basis of the truth I find there? That truth is centered in the

Lord Jesus Christ, as seen in the Bible. There the invisible God is made visible, the inscrutable knowable, the eternal God disclosed in space and time. Do I look to Jesus in order to know God? Do I think of God's attributes by what Jesus shows me of them? If not, I am worshiping an image of God, albeit an image of my own devising. If I look to Jesus, then I can know that I am worshiping the true God, as he has revealed himself. Paul says that although some knew God they nevertheless "did not honor him as God or give thanks to him" (Rom. 1:21). Let us determine that this shall not be true of us. We see God in Jesus. So let us know him as God, love him as God, serve him as God and worship him as God.

10 GOD IN THREE PERSONS

In chapter nine I distinguished between those attributes of God which we partially share—love, wisdom, power and so on—and those which we do not share. The first we can understand. The second we cannot. To a degree we can understand what is meant by God's self-existence, his self-sufficiency and his eternity. We can express them negatively, saying that God has no origins, needs nothing, will never cease to exist and does not change. But we don't understand what they mean in and of themselves. Therefore, the first answers to who God is and what he is like are humbling.

Chapter eleven looks at those attributes that we can better understand. But first, let us look at one more problem area: the Trinity—God, although one, nevertheless exists in three persons, God the Father, God the Son and God the Holy Spirit. The word *Trinity* is not in the Bible. It comes from the Latin word *trinitas,* which means "threeness." But even though the word is not in the Bible, the trinitarian idea is there, and it is most important. It is important because there can be no real blessing either upon ourselves or our work if we neglect any one of the persons of the Godhead.

In the minds of some, the difficulty of understanding how God can be both one and three is reason enough to reject the doctrine outright. Such people cannot understand the Trinity and therefore deny it. Often they complain that theology should be "simple," because simplicity is beautiful, God is beautiful and must therefore be simple and so on. But this is a misunderstanding of reality as well as of the nature of the God revealed to us in the Bible.

Why should reality be simple? Actually, as C. S. Lewis has pointed out in *Mere Christianity*, it is usually the case that reality is odd. "It is not neat, not obvious, not what you expect.... Reality, in fact, is usually something you would not have guessed."[1] This is true for very common things—a table and chair, for example. They seem simple, but if we are to speak of their construction from atoms and of the forces that hold these atoms together, even these supposedly "simple" things go beyond our minds' comprehension. More complex things are even more beyond us. Thus, the maker of the table and chair is more complicated than the things he has made, and God, who made the maker, should be the most complicated and incomprehensible of all.

Three Persons
God has revealed some of his complexity to us in the doctrine of the Trinity. What we know about the Trinity we know only because of God's revelation of it in the Bible, and even then we don't know it well. In fact, so prone are we to make mistakes in dealing with this subject that we must be specially careful lest we go beyond or misrepresent what we find in Scripture.

The first thing we must say is that Christians believe, just as much as Jews believe, that God is one. Because Christians also believe in the Trinity they have been inaccurately accused of believing in three gods, a form of polytheism. It is true that Christians see a plurality within the Godhead, because God himself reveals that it is there. But that is not polytheism. Christians, like believing Jews, are monotheists. That is, we believe in one God. We will recite with the Jew,

> *Hear, O Israel: The LORD our God is one LORD: and you shall love the LORD your God with all your heart, and with all your soul, and with all your might. And these words which I command you this day shall be upon your heart; and you shall teach them diligently to your children, and shall talk of them when you sit in your house, and when you walk by the way, and when you lie down, and when you rise. And you shall bind them as a sign upon your hand, and they shall be as frontlets between your eyes. And you shall write them on the doorposts of your house and on your gates. (Deut. 6:4-9)*

Here in the clearest language is the teaching that God is one and that this teaching should be known by God's people, talked about by them and taught to their children.

The same truth is in the New Testament, which is uniquely Christian. We read that "an idol has no real existence" and that "there is no God but one" (1 Cor. 8:4). We are reminded of the fact that there is but "one God and Father of us all, who is above all and through all and in all" (Eph. 4:6). James says, "You believe that God is one; you do well" (Jas. 2:19).

It has been argued that because the verses which we have quoted from Deuteronomy begin "Hear, O Israel: The LORD our God is *one* LORD" that the Trinity is excluded. But in this very verse the word for "one" is *echad* which means not one in isolation but one in unity. In fact, the word is never used in the Hebrew Bible of a stark singular entity. It is the word used in speaking of one bunch of grapes, for example, or in saying that the people of Israel responded as one people.

After God has brought his wife to him, Adam says, "This at last is bone of my bones and flesh of my flesh; she shall be called Woman, because she was taken out of Man." The text adds, "Therefore a man leaves his father and his mother and cleaves to his wife, and they become one flesh" (Gen. 2:23-24). Again the word is *echad.* It is not suggested that the man and woman were to become one person, but rather that in a divine way they do become one. In a similar but not identical way, God is one God but also existent in three "persons."

One of our difficulties at this point is that we don't have an adequate word in English, or any other language, to express the nature of the different existences within the Godhead. The best word we have is *person,* which comes from the Latin word *persona*—meaning the mask which an actor used when representing some character in a Greek drama. But when we talk of a mask we are already off the track. For we must not think of the persons in God being merely a way in which God from time to time represents himself to human beings. This particular error is known as modalism or Sabellianism, from the name of the man who first popularized it in church history (about the middle of the third century).

The word most often used in the Greek language was *homoousios,* which literally means "one being." But again, this is misleading if we begin to think that there are therefore three distinct beings with different natures within the Godhead. Calvin liked none of these words. He preferred the word *subsistence.* But, while probably quite accurate, nevertheless this word hardly conveys much meaning to most readers in our century.

Actually, the word *person* is all right, as long as we understand what we mean by a person. In common speech the word normally denotes a human being, and therefore one who is uniquely an individual. We have that concept in mind when we speak of depersonalizing someone. But that is not the meaning of the word as used in theology. It is possible to be a person entirely apart from our bodily existence. We may, for example, lose an arm or leg in some accident, yet we will still be a person with all the marks of personality. Moreover, at least according to Christian teaching, even when we die and our bodies decay to ruin we will still be persons. What we are really talking about, then, is a sense of existence expressing itself in knowledge, feelings and a will.

So there are three persons or subsistences within God, each with knowledge, feelings and a will. And yet, even here we are getting off the track. For in the case of God, the knowledge, feelings and will of each person within the Godhead—Father, Son, and Holy Spirit—are identical.

Light, Heat, Air

How can we illustrate that God is one God but that he exists in three persons? It is almost impossible to find a good illustration, though many have been suggested. Some have suggested the idea of a cake which can at the same time be layers, slices and ingredients. The Father could be compared to the ingredients, the Son to the layers (by which God comes down to us), and the Holy Spirit to the slices (by which he is passed around). Another illustration is that of a man who may at the same time be a father, a son and a husband. But the problem with that illustration is that he can only be one of these things to one individual (or, in the case of being a father, to a small number of individuals), while in God's case he is Father, Son and Holy Spirit to all.

Perhaps a better illustration of the Trinity is the illustration of light, heat and air. If you hold your hand out and look at it, each of these three things is present. There is light, because it is only by light that you can see your hand. In fact, even if the darkness of night should descend, there would still be light. There would be infrared light. Although you couldn't see it, it could be picked up by special equipment. There is also heat between your head and your hand. You may prove it by holding out a thermometer. It will vary as you go from a cold room to a warm room or from the outside to indoors. Finally, there is air. You can blow on your hand and feel it. You can wave your hand and thus fan your face.

The point is that each of these three—light, heat and air—is distinct. Each obeys its own laws and may be studied separately. And yet, at the same time it is (at least in a normal earthly setting) impossible to have any one without the others. They are three and yet they are one. Together they make up the environment in which we have our being.

The interesting thing about this illustration is that the Bible speaks of each of these elements in relation to God.

Light: "This is the message we have heard from him and proclaim to you, that God is light and in him is no darkness at all" (1 Jn. 1:5).

Heat: "For our God is a consuming fire" (Heb. 12:29).

Air, breath or wind (the root meaning of the word *Spirit*): "The wind blows where it wills, and you hear the sound of it, but you do not know whence it comes or whither it goes; so it is with every one who is born of the Spirit" (Jn. 3:8).[2]

What the Bible Says

The important point is not whether we can understand the Trinity, even with the help of illustrations, but whether we will believe what the Bible has to say about the Father, Son and Holy Spirit, and about their relationship to each other. What the Bible says may be summarized in the following five propositions:

1. *There is but one living and true God who exists in three persons: God the Father, God the Son and God the Holy Spirit.* We have already looked at this truth in general. We will see it more fully when I talk about the full deity of the Son and Holy Spirit in the other volumes in this series. Here we note a plurality within the Godhead that is suggested even in the pages of the Old Testament, before the Incarnation of the Lord Jesus Christ or the coming of the Holy Spirit upon all God's people. The plurality may be seen, in the first instance, in those passages in which

God speaks about himself in the plural. One example is Genesis 1:26. "Then God said, 'Let us make man in our image, after our likeness.' " Another is Genesis 11:7. "Come, let us go down, and there confuse their language." A third is Isaiah 6:8. "And I heard the voice of the Lord saying, 'Whom shall I send, and who will go for us?' " In other passages a heavenly being termed "the angel of the Lord" is, on the one hand, identified with God and yet, on the other hand, is also distinguished from him. Thus, we read: "The angel of the LORD found her [Hagar] by a spring of water in the wilderness. . . . The angel of the LORD said to her, 'I will so greatly multiply your descendants that they cannot be numbered for multitude.' . . . So she called the name of the LORD who spoke to her, 'Thou art a God of seeing' " (Gen. 16:7, 10, 13). An even stranger case is the appearance of the three angels to Abraham and Lot. The angels are sometimes spoken of as three and sometimes as one. Moreover, when they speak, it is the Lord who, we are told, speaks to Lot and Abraham (Gen. 18).

A final, startling passage is Proverbs 30:4. The prophet Agur is speaking about the nature of Almighty God, confessing his ignorance of him. "Who has ascended to heaven and come down? Who has gathered the wind in his fists? Who has wrapped up the waters in a garment? Who has established all the ends of the earth?" Then comes, "What is his name, and what is his son's name? Surely you know!" In that day the prophet knew only the Father's name, the name Jehovah. Today we know that his Son's name is the Lord Jesus Christ.

2. *The Lord Jesus Christ is fully divine, being the second person of the Godhead who became man.* This, of course, is where the crux of debate on the Trinity is to be found; those who dislike the doctrine dislike it primarily because they are unwilling to give such an exalted position to "the man" Jesus.

Such reluctance is seen first in the teachings of Arius of Alexandria (died A.D. 336). Sabellius, mentioned earlier, tended to merge the persons of the Trinity, so that Father,

Son and Holy Spirit were only temporary manifestations of the one God, assumed for the purposes of our redemption. Arius, whose main work was done just before Sabellius, went to the other extreme. He divided the persons of the Trinity so the Son and the Spirit became less than God the Father. According to Arius, the Son and Spirit were beings willed into existence by God for the purpose of acting as his agents in redemption. Thus, they were not eternal (as God is), and they were not fully divine. Arius used the word *divine* to describe them in some lesser sense than when applying it to the Father. In more recent centuries the same error has been espoused by Unitarians and by some modern cults.

But it is a great error. For if Christ is not fully divine, then our salvation is neither accomplished nor assured. No being less than God himself, however exalted, is able to bear the full punishment of the world's sin.

The deity of the Lord Jesus Christ is taught in many crucial passages. We read "In the beginning was the Word, and the Word was with God, and the Word was God. He was in the beginning with God" (Jn. 1:1-2). That John 1:1-2 speaks of the Lord Jesus Christ is clear from John 1:14, in which we are told that the "Word" of verse 1 "became flesh and dwelt among us." Similarly, Paul writes, "Have this mind among yourselves, which you have in Christ Jesus, who, though he was in the form of God, did not count equality with God a thing to be grasped, but emptied himself, taking the form of a servant, being born in the likeness of men. And being found in human form he humbled himself and became obedient unto death, even death on a cross" (Phil. 2:5-8). The words "did not count equality with God a thing to be grasped, but emptied himself" do not mean that Jesus ceased to be fully God in the Incarnation, as some have maintained, but only that he temporarily laid aside his divine glory and dignity in order to live among us. We remember that it was during the days of his life here that Jesus said, "I and the Father are one"

(Jn. 10:30), and "He who has seen me has seen the Father" (Jn. 14:9).[3]

3. *The Holy Spirit is fully divine.* It is the Lord Jesus Christ who most clearly teaches the nature of the Holy Spirit. In the Gospel of John, Jesus compares the ministry of the coming Holy Spirit to his own ministry. "And I will pray the Father, and he will give you another Counselor, to be with you for ever, even the Spirit of truth, whom the world cannot receive, because it neither sees him nor knows him" (Jn. 14:16-17). This understanding of the Holy Spirit is supported by the fact that distinctly divine attributes are ascribed to him: everlastingness (Heb. 9:14), omnipresence (Ps. 139:7-10), omniscience (1 Cor. 2:10-11), omnipotence (Lk. 1:35) and others.

4. *While each is fully divine, the three persons of the Godhead are related to each other in a way that implies some differences.* Thus, it is usually said in Scripture that the Father (not the Spirit) sent the Son into the world (Mk. 9:37; Mt. 10:40; Gal. 4:4), but that both the Father and the Son send the Spirit (Jn. 14:26; 15:26; 16:7). We don't know fully what such a description of relationships within the Trinity means. But usually it is said that the Son is subject to the Father, for the Father sent him, and that the Spirit is subject to both the Father and the Son, for he is sent into the world by both the Son and Father. However, we must remember that when we speak of subjection we don't mean inequality. Thus, although related to each other in these ways, the members of the Godhead are "the same in substance, equal in power and glory," as the Westminster Shorter Catechism says (Q. 6).

5. *In the work of God the members of the Godhead work together.* It is common among Christians to divide the work of God among the three persons, applying the work of creation to the Father, the work of redemption to the Son and the work of sanctification to the Holy Spirit. A more correct way of speaking is to say that each member of the Trinity cooperates in each work.

One example is the work of *creation*. It is said of God the
Father, "Of old thou didst lay the foundation of the earth,
and the heavens are the work of thy hands" (Ps. 102:25); and
"In the beginning God created the heavens and the earth"
(Gen. 1:1). It is written of the Son, "For in him all things
were created, in heaven and on earth, visible and invisible"
(Col. 1:16); and "All things were made through him, and without him was not anything made that was made" (Jn. 1:3). It is
written of the Holy Spirit, "The spirit of God has made me"
(Job 33:4). In the same way, the *Incarnation* is shown to have
been accomplished by the three persons of the Godhead
working in unity, though only the Son became flesh (Lk. 1:
35). At *the baptism of the Lord* all three were also present: the
Son came up out of the water, the Spirit descended in the
appearance of a dove and the voice of the Father was heard
from heaven declaring, "This is my beloved Son, with whom I
am well pleased" (Mt. 3:16-17). All three persons were present
in the *atonement,* as Hebrews 9:14 declares. "Christ . . .
through the eternal Spirit offered himself without blemish to
God." The *resurrection* of Christ is likewise attributed sometimes to the Father (Acts 2:32), sometimes to the Son (Jn. 10:
17-18) and sometimes to the Holy Spirit (Rom. 1:4).

We are not surprised, therefore, that our salvation as a
whole is also attributed to each of the three persons: "chosen
and destined by God the Father and sanctified by the Spirit
for obedience to Jesus Christ and for sprinkling with his
blood" (1 Pet. 1:2). Nor are we surprised that we are sent forth
into all the world to "make disciples of all nations, baptizing
them in the name of the Father and of the Son and of the Holy
Spirit" (Mt. 28:19).

Threefold Redemption

Again let me note, although we can say meaningful things
about the Trinity (on the basis of God's revelation of them),
the Trinity is still unfathomable. We should be humble before

the Trinity. Someone once asked Daniel Webster, the orator, how a man of his intellect could believe in the Trinity. "How can a man of your mental caliber believe that three equals one?" his assailant chided. Webster replied, "I do not pretend fully to understand the arithmetic of heaven now." Certainly the doctrine of the Trinity does not mean that three equals one. It means rather that God is three in one sense and one in another. But that distinction doesn't really help us to understand the doctrine of the Trinity better. We believe it, not because we understand it, but because the Bible teaches it and because the Spirit himself witnesses within our heart that it is so.

At the same time, we can rejoice in our God, recognizing that he has created us in his image and that he has acted in each person of his being to redeem us. We are ruined by sin. But the triune God has acted to save us. As the Son, he died that we might receive a new spirit, adopting us as sons. As the Holy Spirit, he has entered our lives, giving us a new soul (sometimes called "the new man"). As the Father, he has planned our redemption and will one day raise us from the dead, at which time we will receive a new body and enter into the fullness of life with God.

11

OUR SOVEREIGN GOD

There are qualities in God we will never fully understand. We can speak of God's self-existence, self-sufficiency, eternity and triune nature. Nevertheless we must always recognize that we don't understand them completely, for we are not like God in any of these qualities. We must simply confess that he is God and that we are his creatures. The infinite is beyond our understanding. On the other hand there are qualities of God that we can understand, because to a limited degree we share in them. This is true of most of God's attributes: wisdom, truthfulness, mercy, grace, justice, wrath, goodness, faithfulness and others. It is this category that will occupy us now.

First Things First

Let me begin with God's sovereignty. He has absolute authority and rule over his creation. In order to be sovereign God must also be all-knowing, all-powerful and absolutely free. If he were limited in any one of these areas, he would not be entirely sovereign. Yet the sovereignty of God is greater than any one of the attributes which it contains. Others may seem more important to us—love, for instance. But a little thought will show that the exercise of any of these attributes is made possible only by the sovereignty of God. God might love, for example, but if he were not sovereign, circumstances could thwart his love, making it useless to us. It is the same with God's justice. God may desire to establish justice among human beings, but if he were not sovereign, justice could be frustrated and injustice prevail.

So the doctrine of the sovereignty of God is no mere philosophical dogma devoid of practical value. Rather it is the doctrine that gives meaning and substance to all other doctrines. It is, as Arthur Pink observes, "the foundation of Christian theology . . . the center of gravity in the system of Christian truth—the sun around which all the lesser orbs are grouped."[1] It is also, as we will see, the Christian's strength and comfort amid the storms of this life.

Is God Sovereign?

Of course there are problems in asserting God's rule in relation to a world that has obviously gone its own way. We may grant that God rules heaven. But the earth is an ungodly place. Here God's authority is flouted and sin often prevails. Can we really say that God is sovereign in the midst of such a world? The answer is that if we look at the world alone, obviously not. But if we begin with the Scriptures, as we must do if we would know God, then we can affirm it; for the Bible everywhere declares that God is sovereign. We may not understand that doctrine. We may still wonder why God tolerates sin. But still we won't doubt the doctrine nor retreat from its consequences.

In Scripture the sovereignty of God is so pervasive and important a concept that it is impossible to treat it comprehensively. A few texts, however, will make the doctrine plain.

"Thine, O LORD, is the greatness, and the power, and the glory, and the victory, and the majesty; for all that is in the heavens and in the earth is thine; thine is the kingdom, O LORD, and thou art exalted as head above all . . . thou rulest over all" (1 Chron. 29:11-12). The psalms contain the same teaching. "The earth is the LORD's and the fulness thereof, the world and those who dwell therein" (Ps. 24:1). "Be still, and know that I am God. I am exalted among the nations, I am exalted in the earth!" (Ps. 46:10). "God is the king of all the earth" (Ps. 47:7). The doctrine of the sovereignty of God lies at the root of all admonitions to trust in, praise and commit one's way to him.

In addition to these texts and many others like them, there are also examples of God's rule over the material order. The world of objects and matter obeys those rules which God has set over it. They are the laws of nature or science. We must not think, however, that the so-called laws are absolute and that God is somehow controlled or limited by them; for on some occasions God acts in an unpredictable way to do what we term a miracle.

God showed his sovereignty over nature in dividing the Red Sea so the children of Israel could pass over from Egypt into the wilderness and then by returning the waters to destroy the pursuing Egyptian soldiers. He showed his sovereignty in sending manna to feed the people while they were in the wilderness. On another occasion he sent quails into the camp for meat. God divided the waters of the Jordan River so the people could pass over into Canaan. He caused the walls of Jericho to fall. He stopped the sun in the days of Joshua at Gibeon so that Israel might gain a full victory over her fleeing enemies. In the days of Jesus, God's sovereignty was seen in the feeding of the four and five thousand from a few small loaves and fish, in acts of healing the sick and raising the dead. Eventually, it was seen in the events connected with the crucifixion of Christ and the resurrection.

Other texts show that God's sovereignty extends to the human will and therefore also to human actions. Thus, God hardened Pharaoh's heart so that he refused to let the people of Israel go. On the other hand, he melts some individuals' hearts so that they respond to his love and obey him.

It may be objected, as we noted above, that some men and women nevertheless defy God and disobey him. But this observation cannot overthrow the teaching of the Bible concerning God's rule over his creation, unless the Bible is allowed to be self-contradictory. The explanation of the seeming contradiction is that human rebellion, while it is in opposition to God's express command, falls within his eternal or hidden purpose. That is, God permits sin for his own reasons, knowing in advance that he will bring sin to judgment in the day of his wrath and that in the meantime it will not go beyond the bounds that he has fixed for it. Many things work against the sovereignty of God—from our perspective. But from God's perspective, his decrees are always established. They are, in fact, as the Westminster Shorter Catechism describes them, "his eternal purpose, according to the counsel of his will, whereby, for his own glory, he hath foreordained whatsoever comes to pass."

The Real Problem
The real problem with the sovereignty of God, from a human perspective, is not that the doctrine seems untrue, though there are problems in sorting it out intellectually, but rather that men and women basically do not like this disturbing and humbling aspect of God's character. We might think, if we were to look at the matter superficially, that men and women living in the midst of a chaotic culture would welcome sovereignty. "For what could be better," we might argue, "than knowing that things are really under control, in spite of appearances, and that God is able to work all events out for good eventually?" But this opinion fails to reckon with

humanity's basic rebellion against God seen in our human quest for autonomy.

Rebellion has been characteristic of humankind since the earliest moments in the history of our race. But it is particularly visible in contemporary culture, as R.C. Sproul points out in *The Psychology of Atheism*. Our democratic system, for example, rejects all monarchical authority. "We serve no sovereign here" was a slogan of the American War of Independence. Today, though over two hundred years have gone by, the motif is still with us. So "government of the people" really means "government by myself " or at least by those who are basically like me and agree with me. God, the rightful Lord over all nations as well as over all individuals, is carefully excluded from the decision-making institutions of our national life.

Nor is the church much better, as Sproul also indicates. We often hear the "Savior" characteristics of God stressed—his love, mercy, goodness and so on—but the matter of his lordship is absent. The distortion is particularly clear in evangelism. In modern practice the call to repentance is usually called an "invitation," which one can obviously accept or refuse. It is offered politely. Seldom do we hear presented God's sovereign demand to repent or his demand for total submission to the authority of his appointed king, Christ Jesus.

Today, even in theology, the emphasis in the church's proclamation is on liberation. But sometimes the liberation is from God as well as from "oppressive social structures," as the proponents of liberation theology term it. "In a word," says Sproul, "modern 'liberation' involves a revolt against the sovereign authority of God as members of Church and State join forces in a mutual act of cosmic treason."[2]

The basic reason why women and men do not like the doctrine of God's sovereignty is that they do not want a sovereign God. They wish to be autonomous. So they either deny God's existence entirely, deny this attribute of his existence or else simply ignore him for all practical purposes.

The immediate factor in the current breakdown in respect for authority is the impact of European existentialism through the works of such men as Friedrich Nietzsche, Jean Paul Sartre, Albert Camus and Martin Heidegger. In their works the autonomy of the individual is a dominant philosophical ideal before which all other concepts, including the existence of God, must be eliminated. We find ourselves only when all external restraints are cast off. Only when God is eliminated can we be truly human. But does this work? In Nietzsche's work the ideal figure is the "superman" or *Uebermensch,* the one who creates his own values and who is answerable to no one but himself. But Nietzsche, the inventor of this philosophy, died not as a free person but as a prisoner of his own mind through insanity. The philosophy of existential autonomy is a dead end—worse than that, a disaster. But still it is the dominant philosophy of our age. God is restricting, so he must be cast off—that is the viewpoint. Questions must therefore be answered, not on the basis of a divinely revealed principle of right versus wrong, but on the basis of what the individual or a majority of individuals desire. Sometimes the majority within one particular segment of society stands in opposition to those in other segments.

The problem did not begin with existentialism, however. It began long before that—when Satan confronted the first woman in the garden of Eden by asking her the diabolical question, "Did God say?" and then by suggesting that in disobeying what God said she and her husband would become "as God, knowing good and evil." *As God* is the crucial phrase, for it means to become autonomous. It was the temptation to attempt to replace God in the matter of his sovereignty, as Satan had himself tried to do earlier.

Did the results promised by the serpent follow? Not at all. It is true that the man and woman did learn the difference between good and evil, in a perverted way. They learned by doing evil. But they didn't gain the freedom they wished. Instead they gained bondage to sin, from which only the Lord Jesus Christ through his obedience to the Father was able to deliver both them and us. Human autonomy led to the crucifixion of Christ. "The kings of the earth set themselves, and the rulers take counsel together, against the LORD and his anointed, saying, 'Let us burst their bonds asunder, and cast their cords from us' " (Ps. 2:2-3). True freedom comes by crucifixion _with_ Christ, as the apostle Paul indicates: "I have been crucified with Christ; it is no longer I who live, but Christ who lives in me; and the life I now live in the flesh I live by faith in the Son of God, who loved me and gave himself for me" (Gal. 2:20).

This is a paradox, of course, as Augustine, Luther, Edwards, Pascal and others have pointed out. When individuals rebel against God, they don't achieve freedom. They fall into bondage, because rebellion is sin, and sin is a tyrant. On the other hand, when men and women submit to God, becoming his slaves, they become truly free. They achieve the ability fully to become the special, unique beings that God created them to be.

Blessings of Sovereignty
We find true freedom when we are willing to accept reality as it is (including God's rightful and effective sovereignty over all his creation) and when we allow him to make us into all that he would have us be. The matter of God's sovereignty, far from continuing to be an offense to us, can become a wonderful doctrine from which we derive great blessings.

What are these blessings? First, a realization of God's sovereignty inevitably _deepens our veneration of the living and true God._ Without an understanding and appreciation of these truths, it is questionable whether we know the God of the Old and New Testaments at all. For what is a God whose power is constantly being thwarted by the designs of people and Satan? What kind of a God is he whose sovereignty must be increasingly restricted lest he be imagined to be invading the citadel of our "free will"? Who can worship such a truncated and pitiable deity? Pink says, "A 'god' whose will is resisted, whose designs are frustrated, whose purpose is checkmated, possesses no title to Deity, and so far from being a fit object of worship, merits nought but contempt."[3] On the other hand, a God who truly rules his universe is a God to be joyfully sought after, worshiped and obeyed.

Such is the God whom Isaiah saw: "I saw the Lord sitting upon a throne, high and lifted up; and his train filled the temple. Above him stood the seraphim; each had six wings: with two he covered his face, and with two he covered his feet, and with two he flew. And one called to another and said: 'Holy, holy, holy is the LORD of hosts; the whole earth is full of his glory'" (Is. 6:1-3). Such is the God of the Scriptures. It was a vision of him, not of a lesser god, that transformed Isaiah's ministry.

Second, a knowledge of God in his sovereignty *gives comfort in the midst of trials, temptation or sorrow.* Temptations and sorrows come to Christians and non-Christians alike. The question is: How shall we meet them? Clearly, if we must face them with no clear certainty that they are controlled by God and are permitted for his good purposes, then they are meaningless and life is a tragedy. That is precisely what many existentialists say. But if God is still in control, then such circumstances are known to him and have their purpose.

We don't know all God's purposes, of course. To know that, we would have to be God. Nevertheless, we can know some of them because God reveals them to us. For example, the aged apostle Peter writes to some who had endured great trials, reminding them that the end is not yet—Jesus will return—and that in the meantime God is strengthening and purifying them through their struggles. "In this you rejoice, though now for a little while you may have to suffer various trials, so that the genuineness of your faith, more precious than gold which though perishable is tested by fire, may redound to praise and glory and honor at the revelation of Jesus Christ" (1 Pet. 1:6-7). Similarly, Paul writes to those at Thessalonica who had lost loved ones through death, reminding them that the Lord Jesus Christ will return and will at that time reunite all who are living then with their loved ones. He concludes, "Therefore comfort one another with these words" (1 Thess. 4:18).

Third, an understanding of the sovereignty of God will *provide encouragement and joy in evangelism.* How can one evangelize without such confidence? How can one propose to take a message which is so obviously unpalatable to the natural man or woman and have any hope of moving him or her to accept it, unless God is able to take rebellious sinners and turn them in spite of their own inclinations to faith in Jesus? If God cannot do that, how can any sane human being hope in himself to do it? He would have to be either oblivious to the problem or else ridiculously self-confident. But if God is sovereign in this as in all other matters—if God calls whom he wills and calls "effectively"—then we can be bold in evangelism, knowing that God by grace may use us as channels of his blessing. Indeed, we can know that he will use us. For it is by human testimony that he has determined to bring others to him.

Finally, a knowledge of the sovereignty of God will *afford a deep sense of security.* If we look to ourselves, we have no security at all. The lust of the flesh and eyes, the pride of life, are stronger than we are. Yet, when we look to the strength of our God, we can be confident. Paul writes,

What then shall we say to this? If God is for us, who is against us? ... Who shall separate us from the love of Christ? Shall tribulation, or distress, or persecution, or famine, or nakedness, or peril, or sword? ... No, in all these things we are more than conquerors through him who loved us. For I am sure that neither death, nor life, nor angels, nor principalities, nor things present, nor things to come, nor powers, nor height, nor depth, nor anything else in all creation, will be able to separate us from the love of God in Christ Jesus our Lord. (Rom. 8:31, 35, 37-39)

How can Paul make such statements? Only because he had come to know the sovereign God. To know the true God affords great security even in insecure times.

God Is Able

The Bible is filled from beginning to end with statements of what God is able to do and will do for those who are his people. Here are seven verses which, when put together, cover almost all the fundamental doctrines of Christianity.

1. Hebrews 7:25 in one sense includes all the rest. It tells us that Jesus Christ "is able for all time to save those who draw near to God through him, since he always lives to make intercession for them." Mel Trotter, an evangelist of an earlier generation whom God had called from a life of alcoholism, said that this was his verse; it told of God's ability to save a person "from the guttermost to the uttermost." That is our story also. It covers the past, present and future of salvation.

2. In 2 Timothy 1:12 Paul writes, "For I know whom I have believed and I am sure that he is able to guard until that Day what has been entrusted to me." The metaphor is that of banking, and the verse literally means "God has the power to keep my spiritual deposits." He will not disappoint us.

3. Next, 2 Corinthians 9:8 says, "God is able to provide you with every blessing in abundance, so that you may always have enough of everything and may provide in abundance for every good work." Some Christians think that the salvation of a man or woman by God is for the future only, more or less a "pie in the sky by and by" philosophy. Not so. The Bible tells us that God's grace is available to help us in every good work now. It is in this life that we are to abound in his sufficiency.

4. We are also told that God is able to help us in times of

temptation. The Bible says of Jesus, "Because he himself has suffered and been tempted, he is able to help those who are tempted" (Heb. 2:18). The best commentary on this verse is found in Scripture; we are told elsewhere that although temptation is the common human lot, God does not allow us to be tempted above our capacity to resist it, and, what is more, has provided a means of escape even before the temptation comes upon us (1 Cor. 10:13).

5. Ephesians 3:20 tells us that God is able to help us grow spiritually. It is in the form of a benediction. "Now to him who by the power at work within us is able to do far more abundantly than all that we ask or think, to him be glory in the church and in Christ Jesus to all generations, for ever and ever. Amen."

6. God's ability to save also extends to our bodies. The Lord Jesus Christ "will change our lowly body to be like his glorious body, by the power which enables him even to subject all things to himself" (Phil. 3:21).

7. Finally, in another verse that is also a great benediction, Jude says, "Now to him who is able to keep you from falling and to present you without blemish before the presence of his glory with rejoicing, to the only God, our Savior through Jesus Christ our Lord, be glory, majesty, dominion, and authority, before all time and now and for ever. Amen" (Jude 24-25).

Taken together, these verses declare that God is able to save us for this life and for eternity, to keep us from falling into sin and temptation, to lead us to the best in human experience and to satisfy us completely. Are these things true? Yes ... but for one reason only. They are true because they are the eternal and immutable counsel of the God who is sovereign.

12 HOLY, HOLY, HOLY

"From the standpoint of revelation the first thing which has to be said about God is his sovereignty. But this first point is intimately connected with a second—so closely indeed that we might even ask whether it ought not to have come first: God is the Holy One."[1]

These words by the noted Swiss theologian Emil Brunner reflect the importance of God's holiness. The Bible itself readily confirms Brunner's view since it calls God *holy* more than anything else. *Holy* is the epithet most often affixed to his name. We don't find phrases like "his mighty name," "his wise name" or "his loving name." But we are often reminded of "his holy name." Also we read that God alone is holy. "Who shall not fear and glorify thy name, O Lord? For thou alone art holy" (Rev. 15:4). God is said to be glorious in holiness. "Who is like thee, O LORD, among the gods? Who is like thee, majestic in holiness, terrible in glorious deeds, doing wonders?" (Ex. 15:11). God's holiness is celebrated without ceasing by the seraphim before his throne. Isaiah heard them sing, "Holy, holy, holy is the LORD of hosts; the whole earth is full of his glory" (Is. 6:3). The apostle John heard the seraphim declare, "Holy, holy, holy, is the Lord God Almighty, who was and is and is to come" (Rev. 4:8). God's people are called on to join in these praises. We read, "Sing praises to the LORD, O you his saints, and give thanks to his holy name" (Ps. 30:4).

Because of this emphasis the Christian church prays in the words of the Lord's Prayer, "Hallowed be thy name" (Mt. 6:9 KJV).

Another Category Altogether

To say that the attribute of holiness is important is not to say that we understand it. Of all the attributes of God, in fact, this one is most misconstrued.

One misconception is to think of God's holiness largely in human terms. It is imagined that holiness or righteousness is something that can be graded, more or less. That is, as we look about us we see men and women who come very low on the scale: criminals, perverts and so on. If a perfect score of righteousness is to be considered as, say, one hundred, we might conclude that such persons score in the low teens. Above them are the average individuals of our society. They score in the thirties or forties. Next are the very good people, the judges, philanthropists, and other humanitarians; they are imagined to score possibly in the sixties or seventies—not one hundred, of course, for even they are not as good as they could be. Then, if you push the total on up to a hundred (or beyond, if that is possible), one arrives at the goodness of God.

Most people imagine something like that when they think of God's holiness, if they think of it at all. It is only a perfection of the good in people. But according to the Bible, the holiness of God cannot be placed in the same category as human goodness.

We see the truth of the biblical concept when we study a text such as Romans 10:3, in which the apostle Paul writes of two kinds of righteousness. He says, speaking of the Israel of his day, "For, being ignorant of the righteousness that comes from God, and seeking to establish their own, they did not submit to God's righteousness." This verse distinguishes very clearly between God's righteousness and our righteousness. So even if we were to take all the righteousness of which human beings are capable and heap it all up so that it made a great mountain, it still wouldn't begin to approach the righteousness of God; that is in a different category entirely.

What do we mean when we talk about the holiness of God? To answer that question we must _not_ begin with ethics. Ethics is involved, as we will see. But in its original and most fundamental sense, _holy_ is not an ethical concept at all. Rather it means that which is of the very nature of God and which therefore distinguishes him from everything else. It is what sets God apart from his creation. It has to do with his transcendence.

The fundamental meaning of the word _holy_ is preserved in the meaning of the words _saint_ and _sanctify,_ which are nearly identical to it. _Holy_ comes from the Germanic languages. _Saint_ comes from the Romance languages. But the root meaning of both is identical. In the biblical sense, a saint is not a person who has achieved a certain level of goodness (as most people think), but rather one who has been "set apart" by God. Saints are the "called-out ones" who make up God's church. The same idea is also present when, as in Exodus 40, the Bible refers to the sanctification of objects. In that chapter Moses is instructed to sanctify the altar and basin in the midst of the tabernacle. The chapter does not refer to any intrinsic change in the nature of the stones; they are not made righteous. It merely indicates that they were to be set apart for a special use. Jesus prays, saying, "I consecrate [or sanctify] myself, that they also may be consecrated in truth" (Jn. 17:19). The verse does not mean that Jesus makes himself more righteous, for he already was righteous. It means that he separated himself to a special task, the task of providing salvation for all people by his death.

Holiness, then, is the characteristic of God that sets him apart from his creation. In this, holiness has at least four elements.

The first is *majesty*. Majesty is "dignity," "authority of sovereign power," "stateliness" or "grandeur." It is the proper characteristic of monarchs and is, of course, supremely the attribute of that One who is Monarch over all. Majesty is the dominant element in the visions of God in his glory seen both in the Old Testament and the New. The element of majesty links the idea of holiness to sovereignty.

A second element in the idea of holiness is *will*, the will of a personality. Apart from it the idea of holiness becomes abstract, impersonal and static, rather than concrete, personal and active. Moreover, if we ask what God's will is predominantly set on, the answer is that it is set on proclaiming himself as the "Wholly Other," whose glory must on no account be diminished because of human arrogance and willful rebellion. In the element of will the idea of holiness comes quite close to the "jealousy" of God, which modern man finds so repugnant.

"I the LORD your God am a jealous God" (Ex. 20:5). Rightly understood, the idea of jealousy is central to any true concept of God. It is, as Brunner points out, analogous to a proper jealousy within marriage. A married person ought not to allow any third person to enter into the inner relationship. Similarly, God rejects every attack on his sole rights as Lord of his creation. "The holiness of God is therefore not only an absolute difference of nature, but it is an active self-differentiation, the willed energy with which God asserts and maintains the fact that He is Wholly Other against all else. The absoluteness of this difference becomes the absoluteness of his holy will, which is supreme and unique." [2]

In simpler terms, the holiness of God means that God is not indifferent to how men and women regard him. He does not go his solitary way heedless of their rejection of him. Rather, he wills and acts to see that his glory is recognized. Recognition will come now, in each individual case, or it will become true for each in the day of God's judgment.

A third element in the idea of holiness is the element of *wrath*. Wrath is an essential part of God's holiness, but we must not compare it to an emotional, human reaction to something, a reaction which we normally think of as anger. The wrath of God is not at all like any emotion we know in human experience. It is, rather, that necessary and proper stance of the holy God to all that opposes him. It means that he takes the matter of being God seriously, so seriously that he will not allow any thing or personality to aspire to his place. When Satan sought to do that, Satan was judged (and will yet be judged). When men and women refuse to take the place that God has given to them, they will be judged also.

A final element in the idea of holiness is one we mentioned earlier: *righteousness*. Righteousness is involved in holiness, not because it is the best category by which holiness may be understood, but because, having spoken of the will of God, we immediately go on to see that what God wills is righteousness or holiness in its ethical sense. In other words, when we ask, "What is right? What is moral?" we answer the questions not by appealing to some independent moral standard, as if there could be a standard for anything apart from God, but rather by appealing to the will and nature of God himself. The right is what God is and reveals to us.

The nature of God is an essential foundation for any true or lasting morality. Consequently, where God is not acknowledged, morality (however much talked about) inevitably declines, just as it is doing in contemporary Western civilization. It is the desire to obey God that ultimately makes ethical behavior possible.

The Tabernacle

We have a dramatization of the holiness of God in the laws given for the building of the Jewish tabernacle. On one level, the tabernacle was constructed to teach the immanence of God, the truth that God is always present with his people. But on the other hand, it also taught that God is separated from his people because of his holiness and their sin, and can therefore be approached only in the way he determines.

We must not think that the Jewish people had any more understanding of the holiness of God than we naturally do, for they did not. It was necessary for God to teach them about it. The point of the tabernacle was that a sinful man or woman could not simply "barge in" upon the Holy One. God was understood to have dwelt symbolically within the innermost chamber of the tabernacle, known as the "Holy of Holies." People could not go in there. A Greek could enter any of the temples of Greece and pray before the statue of the pagan god or goddess. A Roman could enter any of the temples of Rome. But a Jew could not enter the Holy of Holies. In fact, only one person could ever go in; that was the high priest of Israel; and even he could go in only once a year and that only after having first made sacrifices for himself and the people in the outer courtyard. The Holy of Holies (the innermost chamber of the tabernacle) was separated from the Holy Place (the outer chamber of the tabernacle) by a thick veil.

Nor was that all. Just as there was a veil between the Holy of Holies and the Holy Place, that is, dividing these two chambers within the tabernacle, so there was another thick veil separating the Holy Place from the outer courtyard. And then there was a third veil closing off the entrance of the courtyard from the surrounding camp of the Israelites.

The meaning of the word *veil* is to "separate" or (later) to "hide." So the meaning of the veils was that God, even though he chose to dwell with his people, was nevertheless separated from them or hidden from them because of his holiness and their sin. Communion with God was to be only within the Holy of Holies. But in order to enter, three curtains had to be passed, each of which added to the sense of the enormous gulf which exists between God and humanity: first, the curtain between the outer camp and the courtyard; second, the covering of the entrance to the Holy Place; third, the curtain separating the Holy Place from the innermost chamber. Likewise, in order to enter the Holy of Holies, the high priest had to perform a sacrifice at the brazen altar in the courtyard, wash at the basin in the courtyard, and then pass through the Holy Place in the light of the seven-branched golden candlestick and through the incense which was always burning upon an altar within that room.

What would happen if a man or woman should ignore these barriers? The answer is that he or she would immediately be consumed, as some who entered were. The wrath of God would flame out against that sin which sought thus to intrude upon or compromise God's holiness. As we recognize his holiness we begin to understand something of human sinfulness and the necessity for Christ's atoning death on the cross.

Permanent Trauma

The holiness of God is another attribute that makes God undesirable and even threatening. We have already pointed out that men and women don't like the sovereignty of God because it is a threat to their desire for sovereignty. They do not find a sovereign God desirable. Negative reaction is even more apparent in regard to God's holiness.

Here we are greatly assisted by a careful analysis of the idea of the *holy* by the German theologian Rudolf Otto. Otto has written a book, called in German *Das Heilige* and in English *The Idea of the Holy,* in which he seeks to understand the specific, nonrational or superrational nature of religious experience from a phenomenological perspective. The superrational element Otto calls the "numinous" or the "holy." There is a great deal of difference between the numinous or holy (as an abstract conception) in the non-Christian religions and the Holy One (as personal) within Judaism and Christianity. But as far as it goes, the analysis is quite helpful, for it shows that men and women find the true God threatening.

In his analysis Otto distinguishes three elements in the holy. The first is *awefulness,* by which he means "that which is profoundly awe-inspiring." We use the word *awful* to mean "extremely bad" or "terrible," but this is a different idea. The awefulness of the holy is that which is so awe-inspiring that it produces fear or trembling in the worshiper. The second element is *overpoweringness.* Supreme and majestic power inevitably engenders a sense of impotence and general worthlessness in the worshiper. The final element is *energy,* by which Otto speaks of the dynamic element present in the encounter.

The point is that the experience of confronting the Holy is supremely threatening. The worshiper is drawn to the Holy, but at the same time he is terrified by it. The awe-inspiring, overpowering energy of the Holy threatens to destroy him.

We should notice that we find the same phenomenon in the Bible also, although the Bible goes on to explain it, as non-Christians do not. The account of Job is an example. Job had suffered the loss of his possessions, family and health. When his friends came to convince him that his loss was because of some sin, either recognized or hidden, Job stoutly defended himself against their accusations. He was right to do so, for Job was suffering as an upright man. "Have you considered my servant Job, that there is none like him on earth, a blameless and upright man, who fears God and turns away from evil?" (Job 1:8). Obviously, if anyone could have stood before the holiness of God, it was Job. Yet, toward the end of the book, after God came to Job with a series of questions and statements designed to teach something of his true majesty to this suffering servant, Job was left nearly speechless and in a state of collapse. He replied to God, "Behold, I am of small account; what shall I answer thee? . . . therefore I despise myself, and repent in dust and ashes" (Job 40:4; 42:6).

We see the same phenomenon in Isaiah who received a vision of the Lord "sitting upon a throne, high and lifted up." He heard the praise of the seraphim. But the effect upon Isaiah, far from being a cause for self-satisfaction or pride that such a vision had been granted to him, was actually devastating. He responded, "Woe is me! For I am lost; for I am a man of unclean lips, and I dwell in the midst of a people of unclean lips; for my eyes have seen the King, the LORD of hosts!" (Is. 6:5). Isaiah saw himself as ruined or undone. Only when a coal was taken from the altar and used to purge his lips was he able to stand upright again and respond affirmatively to God's call to him for service.

Habakkuk also had a vision of God. He had been distressed with the ungodliness in the world around him and had wondered how the ungodly could rightly triumph over the person who was more righteous. The prophet then entered into his watchtower and waited for God's answer. When God answered, Habakkuk was overcome with dread. "I hear, and my body trembles, my lips quiver at the sound; rottenness enters into my bones, my steps totter beneath me" (Hab. 3:16). Habakkuk was a prophet. But even so, a confrontation with God was shattering.

Similarly, although the glory of God was veiled in the person of Jesus Christ, from time to time those who were Christ's disciples perceived who he was, ever so slightly, and had a similar reaction. Thus, after Peter had recognized the glory of God in Christ's miracle in granting a great catch of fish in Galilee, Peter responded, "Depart from me, for I am a sinful man, O Lord" (Lk. 5:8).

When the apostle John received a revelation of Christ's glory, seeing the risen Lord standing in the midst of the seven golden candlesticks, he "fell at his feet as though dead" and rose only after the Lord had touched him and given him a commission to write the book of Revelation. John could stand before the Lord only after he had experienced something akin to a resurrection.

That is what it means to come face to face with the Holy. It is not a pleasant experience. It is profoundly threatening, for the Holy cannot coexist in the same space with the unholy. God must destroy the unholy or else purge out the sin. Moreover, if this is true for the best people, for those whom God has chosen to be his prophets and whom even he calls "righteous," how much more true is it of those who are antagonistic to God? To them the experience is totally overwhelming. As a result they resist, try to make light of or run away from God. Tozer has written, "The moral shock suffered by us through our mighty break with the high will of heaven has left us all with a permanent trauma affecting every part of our nature."[3] He is right. Consequently, men and women will not come to God, and that which should be their great joy is abhorrent to them.

A Holy People

So what do we do, we who are sinful and yet are confronted with the holy God? Do we simply go our own way? Do the best we can? Turn our backs on the Holy? If it were not for the fact that God has chosen to do something about our predicament, that would be all we could do. But the glory of Christianity is its message that the holy God has done something. He has done what was needed. He has made for us a way into his presence through the Lord Jesus Christ, as a result of which the unholy becomes holy and is enabled to dwell with him.

Here we may go back to the illustration provided by the wilderness tabernacle. The tabernacle was intended to teach the great gulf that lay between God in his holiness and human beings in their sin. But it also taught the way by which that gulf could be bridged. In Old Testament times that way was symbolic. It was by the sacrifice of animals in which the sin of the people was symbolically transferred to the innocent victim, which then died in the worshipers' place. That was why the high priest was required to perform a sacrifice first for himself and then for the people before he could enter into the Holy of Holies on the Day of Atonement. But although the symbolism was important and vivid, it wasn't the death of the animals, however many, that actually purged away sin. The true and only atonement was to be provided by the Lord Jesus Christ who, as the perfect Lamb of God, died in place of sinners. Moreover, it was not only the sacrifices that prefigured his work. It was each part of the tabernacle, the altar, the basin, the candlesticks, the incense, the shewbread within the Holy Place and everything else. In other words he is the One through whom we are washed from sin, he is the light of the world, he is the bread of life, he is the basis of worship through prayer, as well as our once-and-for-all sufficient sacrifice.

And Christ is truly sufficient. At the moment when he bore our sin and was therefore judicially separated from the presence of the Father in our place—in that moment God himself tore the veil of the temple in two from top to bottom, thereby indicating that the way into his presence, into the Holy of Holies, is now open for all who will come to him through faith in Christ, as he requires. To those who will come, God then grants a measure of his own holiness in two senses. We will never be holy in the sense of the "Wholly Other," as he is. But we are first separated to him through Christ, as his holy ones, and then made righteous practically and increasingly as his nature gradually transforms our being.

There will be several consequences for those who come to the knowledge of the Holy. First, they will learn to hate sin. We don't naturally hate sin. In fact, the opposite is true. We generally love sin and are loath to part with it. But we must learn to hate sin, or else we will learn to hate God who requires a holy life from those who are Christ's followers. We see a great tension during the lifetime of the Lord Jesus Christ. Some saw his holiness, came to hate sin and became his followers. Others saw him, came to hate him and eventually crucified him.

Second, those who have come to the knowledge of the Holy One through faith in the Lord Jesus Christ will learn to love righteousness and strive for it. Such individuals often need urging. The apostle Peter wrote to those in his day saying, "But as he who called you is holy, be holy yourselves in all your conduct; since it is written, 'You shall be holy, for I am holy' " (1 Pet. 1:15-16). It does not say "Be holy, *as* I am holy." None of us could do that. We cannot be holy in the same sense that God is holy. But we can be holy in the area of a righteous and upright walk before him.

Third, we must look to the day when God will be fully known in his holiness by all men and women, and we can rejoice in anticipation of that day. If we had not come to God through faith in Christ, that day would be terrible. It would mean the exposure of our sin and judgment. Having come, it means rather the completion of our salvation in that we shall be made like Jesus. We shall be like him, in holiness and in every other way, "for we shall see him as he is" (1 Jn. 3:2).

13

THE GOD WHO KNOWS

The unique quality of God's knowledge is its totality or perfection: his *omniscience* is the proper theological term. Omniscience involves not only God's knowledge of us but also his knowledge of nature, the past, present and future. It involves everything that we can possibly imagine and much more besides. It is a knowledge that God has always had and will always have. There is no need for him to learn. In fact, if we are to take the scope of his knowledge at full value, it is necessary to say that God has never learned and cannot learn, for he already knows and has always known everything.

God's omniscience is seen in Isaiah's questionings of a rebellious nation. "Who has directed the Spirit of the LORD, or as his counselor has instructed him? Whom did he consult for his enlightenment, and who taught him the path of justice, and taught him knowledge, and showed him the way of understanding?" (Is. 40:13-14). The answer clearly is no one. God is infinitely above his creation in all knowledge and understanding. Similarly, the Lord himself speaks to Job out of the whirlwind. "Who is this that darkens counsel by words without knowledge? Gird up your loins like a man, I will question you, and you shall declare to me. Where were you when I laid the foundation of the earth? Tell me, if you have understanding. Who determined its measurements—surely you know! Or who stretched the line upon it? On what were its bases sunk, or who laid its cornerstone, when the morning stars sang together, and all the sons of God shouted for joy?" (Job 38:2-7). Once again, the answer is that next to the knowledge of God, which is perfect, human knowledge is near zero.

The knowledge of God extends to the most intimate knowledge of the individual. "I know their works and their thoughts," said God to Isaiah, referring to the Jewish people (Is. 66:18). David declared, "O LORD, thou hast searched me and known me! Thou knowest when I sit down and when I rise up; thou discernest my thoughts from afar. Thou searchest out my path and my lying down, and art acquainted with all my ways. Even before a word is on my tongue, lo, O LORD, thou knowest it altogether" (Ps. 139:1-4). The author of Hebrews writes, "Before him no creature is hidden, but all are open and laid bare to the eyes of him with whom we have to do" (Heb. 4:13).

It is impossible to overstate the qualities of God's knowledge. As Thomas Watson observed years ago, God's knowledge is *primary,* for he is the pattern and source of all knowledge from which others merely borrow; his knowledge is *pure,* for it is not contaminated by either the object or its sin; his knowledge is *facile,* for it is without any difficulty; it is *infallible;* it is *instantaneous;* it is entirely *retentive.* God is perfect in his knowledge.

Staring and Uneasiness

We might think that God's omniscience would be comforting to us in our natural state, for the belief that perfect knowledge exists (even though we don't possess it ourselves) should make the world less threatening. Actually, the opposite is true. To acknowledge that there is a God who knows everything about everything is also to acknowledge that such a God knows us. And because we don't want some things about us to be known, we hide it—not only from others but also from ourselves as much as possible. A God who thoroughly knows us is unsettling.

Arthur W. Pink notes that the thought of divine omniscience "fills us with uneasiness."[1] A. W. Tozer observes, "In the divine omniscience we see set forth against each other the terror and fascination of the Godhead. That God knows each person through and through can be a cause of shaking fear to the man that has something to hide—some unforsaken sin, some secret crime committed against man or God."[2] But it is not just some other person about whom Tozer is speaking. It is descriptive of the entire race, and therefore of us. All have rebelled against God and thus fear exposure.

No one has documented our fear of being exposed more carefully in recent years than R.C. Sproul in _The Psychology of Atheism._ Sproul devotes a chapter to the theme of "God and Nakedness" and analyzes the fear modern people have of being exposed, first to others and then also to God. The first object of his analysis is the work of Jean Paul Sartre. Sartre has spoken of the fear of being beneath the gaze of someone else. We don't mind staring at another, for instance. But the moment we become aware that another is staring at us we become embarrassed, confused and fearful, and our behavior alters. We hate the experience and do whatever we can to avoid it. If we can't avoid it, the experience becomes intolerable.

In what is perhaps Sartre's best-known work, the play _No Exit,_ four characters are confined in a room with nothing to do but talk to and stare at each other. It is a symbol of hell. In the closing lines of the play this becomes quite clear as Garcin stands at the mantelpiece stroking a bronze bust. He says,

Yes, now's the moment: I'm looking at this thing on the mantel-piece, and I understand that I'm in hell. I tell you, everything's been thought out beforehand. They knew I'd stand at the fireplace stroking this thing of bronze, with all those eyes intent on me. Devouring me. (He swings round abruptly.) *What? Only two of you? I thought there were more; many more.* (Laughs.) *So this is hell. I'd never have believed it. You remember all we were told about the torture chambers, the fire and brimstone, the "burning marl." Old wives' tales! There's no need for red-hot pokers. Hell is –other people!*[3]

The final stage directive says that the characters slump down onto their respective sofas, the laughter dies away and they "gaze" at each other.

In Sartre's philosophy this fear of being under the gaze of another is reason for doing away with God; for beneath God's gaze we are reduced to objects and have our humanity destroyed. The point of interest here, however, is the fear of exposure. Where does it come from if not from a real and merited guilt arising from our rebellion against the only sovereign and holy God of the universe?

Sproul next analyzes Julius Fast's book *Body Language.* This book is a study of how human beings communicate nonverbally by various body positions, gestures, tilts of the head, liftings of the eyebrow and so forth. Fast points out that one can stare at an object for very long periods. One can stare at animals. But to stare at another person is unacceptable behavior because, if a glance is held too long, it provokes either embarrassment or hostility or both. The fact that we have doors, window shades, clothes and shower curtains demonstrates our desire and need for privacy.

Third, Sproul deals with Desmond Morris's *The Naked Ape,* another popular work. The "naked ape" is, of course, the human being. The title of the book as well as its content highlight the uniqueness of humans in their nakedness. We are naked animals, having no hair for a covering, but we are ashamed in our nakedness and seek to hide ourselves from the gaze of other persons.

Fourth, Sproul mentions the Danish philosopher and writer Sören Kierkegaard, noting that he "is sharply critical of the person who lives merely on the 'aesthetic' or 'spectator' plane of life, operating within the context of the concealment of a masquerade," while he himself "preserved an island of hiddenness for himself and for all men." He knew that "solitude affords a place of hiddenness that is necessary for the human subject."[4]

What emerges from these modern expressions is a strange ambivalence. On the one hand, women and men long to be known. The modern proof is in the popularity of encounter sessions, psychiatry, talk shows and X-rated movies. But in a far deeper way men and women fear such exposure, for they are ashamed of what is there to be seen—by other people and by God. With others there are always ways to achieve a covering. We wear clothes, for example. On the psychological level, we carefully guard what we say so that only those things about us that we wish to be known are known. Sometimes we put on a false front entirely. But what are we to do in regard to God before whom "all hearts are open, all desires known"? There is nothing to be done. Nothing can be done. Consequently, it is an awareness of the knowledge of God, as well as his sovereignty and holiness, that produces anxiety and even dread in fallen women and men.

Covered with Robes of Righteousness

Dread of God's knowledge is not a normal experience for Christians. But before we see what it does mean to them we must determine why it has ceased to be fearful. Here the experience of Adam and Eve is enlightening. Adam and Eve had sinned, and when they sinned they recognized that they were naked. They had been naked beforehand in a purely physical sense. But they had not yet sinned and so "were not ashamed"

(Gen. 2:25). After they became sinners, their nakedness became something more than merely physical. It had become a psychological nakedness connected to their moral guilt. They were guilty, before one another and also before God.

What happened? God came "walking in the garden" to confront them in their nakedness. He exposed their sin, for sin cannot be hidden in his presence. But then he did something tremendous. He clothed them, using skins from animals which he himself sacrificed.

This is the message of Christianity: that we can be known and yet clothed at the same time. Yet being clothed is not accomplished ultimately with the skins of animals. The clothing of Adam and Eve was only a symbol, an acted parable, of what was to come for all when God sent Jesus Christ to die for our sin so that guilt might be removed. On the basis of his perfect and atoning sacrifice, God would then clothe all who believe in Christ with the Lord's own righteousness. Because of Christ's work, God no longer looks on us as sinners but as those who have become righteous in Christ. Now we can stand before him rather than hide. It is not because God has been ignorant of our sin or has refused to care about it, but because he has known about it and has dealt with it perfectly. Now we can cry with Isaiah, "I will greatly rejoice in the LORD, my soul shall exult in my God; for he has clothed me with the garments of salvation, he has covered me with the robe of righteousness, as a bridegroom decks himself with a garland, and as a bride adorns herself with her jewels" (Is. 61:10).

Reasons for Joy

The omniscience of God is a cause of uneasiness and even dread for those who do not have their sin covered with the righteousness of Christ. But for three reasons this omniscience is a great blessing and a cause for joy among Christians.

First, because God knows all things, he knows the *worst about us* and yet has loved us and saved us. In human relationships we often fear that something in us might come to light to break the relationship. Otherwise why would we be so careful to put on our best face with other people? But God already knows the worst about us and nevertheless continues to demonstrate his love. He "knows our frame" and "remembers that we are dust" (Ps. 103:14). We needn't fear that something within us will rise up to startle God, that some forgotten skeleton will come tumbling out of our closet to expose our shameful past or that some informer will speak out against us to bring shame. Nothing can happen that isn't already known to God.

One writer links this sense of security to the ministry of the Holy Spirit within us.

> _Let us take comfort that the Holy Spirit is not dwelling within us as a spy to discover our infirmities and to report them to God for condemnation. The Holy Spirit knows that Christ has been condemned in our place, and he has come within us as the bookkeeper and paying teller of God, to remind us ever of our credit balance, and to give us the fruits of our inheritance in order that we may live in the triumph purchased for us._[5]

Second, not only does God know the worst about us, he also knows _the best about us,_ even though that best may be unknown to any other person. There are times in our lives when we do very well at something and yet find that we go unnoticed. Or we do as well as we possibly can but we fail. What we have done is therefore totally misinterpreted. Perhaps things go in a way we didn't intend. Then people say—even our friends—"How could so-and-so do a thing like that? I would have thought better of him." They don't know the situation, nor do they know our hearts. They are critical, and nothing we can do or say seems to change their opinion. What then? There is comfort in knowing that God, who knows all things, also knows us and knows that we really did do the best of which we were capable. And he doesn't judge us. He doesn't condemn us.

A father is teaching his one-year-old daughter to walk. She

is trying but she falls down. He puts her back on her feet and she falls down again. So he gets angry. He screams and shouts, "You're a dumb child. I'm a good teacher but you're not learning." When she falls the third time he spanks her for it. Obviously we would think very poorly of that kind of father. On the other hand, we would think well of a father who says, "Don't worry about it. You fell down, but you'll walk someday. I know you're doing the very best you can." Our God is like the second of the two. He knows our weaknesses and sin, but he also knows when we are trying, and he is patient.

Third, God knows *what he is going to make of us.* That is, he knows the end we have been made for and he is most certainly going to bring us to it in his own proper time. That end is spelled out in Romans 8:29. Most Christians know the verse that comes immediately before, Romans 8:28. It is a reassuring promise: "We know that in everything God works for good with those who love him, who are called according to his purpose." But it is a pity that very few have gone on to learn the next verse because it tells what the "purpose" mentioned in verse 28 is. "For those whom he foreknew he also predestined to be conformed to the image of his Son, in order that he might be the first-born among many brethren." God is determined to make us like Jesus Christ. That is his purpose in redemption, and it is in this context that Romans 8:28 was written. Redemption begins with God's electing foreknowledge of his own people, his predestination of them to be conformed to Christ's image—his choice of material and the blueprint. Redemption further includes his call of these elected ones to salvation, their justification through the work of Christ and their glorification as a result of which God's purposes with them are finally and totally achieved.

We get discouraged in the Christian life, and with good cause. We take a step forward and fall half a step back. We succeed once, but then we fail twice. We overcome temptation, but we also fall in temptation, sometimes over and over again. We say, "Oh, I'm not making progress at all. I'm doing worse this year than last year. God must be discouraged with me." But God isn't discouraged with us. That is the point. God knows everything. So while it's true that he is fully aware of our failures and victories, few as the victories may be, he is also aware of far more than that. He is aware of what we will one day be when by his grace we are fully conformed to the image of Jesus Christ. It is a sure thing. So we should take confidence in that, even though the discouragements are many and real. We have a great destiny; in its light all the vaunted achievements of our age and our personal achievements fade into virtual insignificance.

There are other areas in which God's omniscience affects our lives. First, if God is the God of all knowledge, then we should learn the importance of knowledge. We are made in the image of God. One of the things that means is that we can learn to think God's thoughts after him and share his knowledge. We can possess true knowledge in the same sense although not to the same degree that God possesses knowledge. There is value in study and learning.

Second, hypocrisy is foolishness. We may try to fool other people about what we're really like, and even succeed up to a point. But we cannot fool God. Therefore, when we stand before him exposed in our sin but covered by Christ's righteousness, then we can stand before anybody never fearing that they might come to know us as we really are. And we can be bold to do the right thing, whether or not it is misunderstood or ridiculed. We can be women and men of our word. We can let our Yes be Yes and our No be No because God knows us. We don't have to pretend to be something we're not.

Finally, we can be encouraged in difficulties. Job went through great difficulties, but still he said, "He knows the way that I take; when he has tried me, I shall come forth as gold" (Job 23:10). Because God knows, believers can rest. We can pray, for we can be assured that no prayer, no cry for help, not even a sigh or a tear escapes the notice of him who sees deep into our hearts. Sometimes we may even fail to pray. But "before they call, I will answer; while they are yet speaking I will hear" (Is. 65:24). All that is needed is that we take these truths down off the high shelf of theology and put them to work as we live our daily lives.

14 GOD WHO CHANGES NOT

The unchangeableness of God is linked to his eternity (which was considered briefly in chapter nine), but they are not identical. The eternity of God means that God has always existed and always will exist; nothing comes before him, nothing after. The unchangeableness of God (immutability) means that God is always the same in his eternal being.

We can readily understand this. Yet this quality is one that separates the Creator from even the highest of his creatures. God is unchangeable while no other part of his creation is. All that we know changes. The material world changes, and not merely in a circular sense, as the Greeks envisioned it—so that all things eventually return to what they were—but rather in the sense of running down, as science indicates. For example, although its decay is spread over a long period of time and is hard to notice, the sun constantly dissipates its energy and will eventually cool. The earth also runs down. Highly complex and active elements such as radioactive materials decay to less active ones. The varied and abundant resources of this earth are exhaustible. Species of life can become extinct and many have. On the individual level, men and women are born, grow, age and eventually die. Nothing that we know lasts forever.

In human terms mutability is due to the fact that we are fallen creatures and are separated from God. The Bible speaks of the wicked as being "like the tossing sea; for it cannot rest" (Is. 57:20). Jude speaks of them as "waterless clouds, carried along by winds" and as "wandering stars," without a sure orbit (Jude 12-13). Surely the moral dimension of the variableness of humanity is nowhere better indicated than in the reaction of the masses to the Lord Jesus Christ. One week they were crying out, "Hosanna! Blessed be he who comes in the name of the Lord, even the King of Israel!" The next week they were shouting, "Away with him, crucify him!"

Human nature cannot be relied on, but God can be relied on. He is unchangeable. His nature is always the same. His will is invariable. His purposes are sure. God is the fixed point in a churning and decaying universe for those who truly know him. After James has spoken of human sin and error he adds that "every good endowment and every perfect gift is from above, coming down from the Father of lights with whom there is no variation or shadow due to change" (Jas. 1:17). The same perspective is shared by the prophet Malachi, who observes in a verse that comes toward the very end of the Old Testament, "I the LORD do not change; therefore you, O sons of Jacob, are not consumed" (Mal. 3:6).

Not for the Better or the Worse

Each of the above verses speaks of the immutability of God in his essential being. That is, being perfect, he never differs from himself. For a moral being to change, it would be necessary to change in one of two directions. Either the change is from something worse to something better, or else it is from something better to something worse. It should be evident that God can move in neither of these directions. God cannot change for the better, for that would mean that he had been imperfect beforehand. If we are talking about righteousness, for example, it would mean that he had been less than righteous and therefore sinful. If we are talking about knowledge, it would mean that he had not known everything and was therefore ignorant. On the other hand, God cannot change for the worse. In that case he would become less than he once was, becoming sinful or imperfect.

The immutability of God as presented in Scripture, however, is not the same thing as the immutability of "god" talked about by the Greek philosophers. In Greek thought immutability meant not only unchangeability but also the inability to be affected by anything in any way. The Greek word for this, the primary characteristic of "god," was _apatheia_, from which we get our word "apathy." Apathy means indifference, but the Greek term goes beyond that idea. It means a total inability to feel any emotion whatever. The Greeks believed "god" possessed this quality because we would otherwise have power over him to the degree that we could move him to anger or joy or grief. He would cease to be absolute and sovereign. So the "god" of the philosophers (though not of the more popular mythologies) was lonely, isolated and compassionless.

That makes good philosophy of course. It is logical. But it is not what God reveals about himself in the Scriptures, and so we must reject it, however logical it may seem. The biblical perspective tells us that God is indeed immutable, but that he nevertheless notices and is affected by the obedience, plight or sin of his creatures.

Brunner writes,

> _If it be true that there really is such a fact as the Mercy of God and the Wrath of God, then God, too, is "affected" by what happens to his creatures. He is not like that divinity of Platonism who is unconcerned, and therefore unmoved, by all that happens upon the earth,_

*but goes his way in heaven without looking around, without taking
into consideration what is happening on earth. God does "look
around"–he does care what happens to men and women–he is concerned about the changes on earth.*[1]

A primary example is seen in the Lord Jesus Christ who,
though he was God, nevertheless wept over the city of Jerusalem and at the tomb of Lazarus.

Disturbing and Comforting

God's immutability also applies to his attributes. The Westminster Shorter Catechism defines God as "a Spirit, infinite,
eternal and unchangeable in his being, wisdom, power, holiness, justice, goodness and truth." God is the possessor of all
knowledge and wisdom, and he will always possess all wisdom.
He is sovereign and will always be sovereign. He is holy and
will always be holy. He is just and will always be just, good and
will always be good, truthful and will always be truthful. Nothing that happens will ever diminish God in these or any of his
attributes.

This truth has two faces: it is disturbing to those who are in
rebellion against God and it is comforting to those who have
come to know him through Christ. The first is evident from
what we have been saying in the last three chapters. If it is true
that the sovereignty, holiness and omniscience of God are un-
likable concepts to the natural man, then it is clear that the
fact that God will not change in any of these areas is even more
disturbing. The unsaved person would not be so troubled by
God's sovereignty if he could think that one day God would
become less sovereign and the individual more autonomous.
It would be conceivable that he, or the human race, could replace God one day. Again, he would not be so bothered by
thoughts of God's holiness if it could be imagined that in time
God might become less holy, calling what he now regards as
sin, not sin, and ignoring the guilty. Or, if God could forget,
then the evil we do would not be so troublesome; given time,

it might fade from God's memory. But the immutability of God means that God will always be sovereign, always be holy, always be omniscient. Consequently all things must be brought to light and be judged before him.

Another side of this doctrine faces the believer. To us it is a great comfort. In this world people forget us, even when we have worked hard and been a service to them. They change their attitude toward us as their own needs and circumstances dictate. Often they are unjust (as we are also). But God is not like that. Rather, his attitude toward us now is the same as it was in the farthest reaches of eternity past and will be in the farthest reaches of eternity to come. The Father loves us to the end, as it was said of Jesus: "When Jesus knew that his hour had come to depart out of this world to the Father, having loved his own who were in the world, he loved them _to the end_" (Jn. 13:1).

Tozer writes of the comfort found in God's immutability.

What peace it brings to the Christian's heart to realize that our heavenly Father never differs from himself. In coming to him at any time we need not wonder whether we shall find him in a receptive mood. He is always receptive to misery and need, as well as to love and faith. He does not keep office hours nor set aside periods when he will see no one. Neither does he change his mind about anything. Today, this moment, he feels toward his creatures, toward babies, toward the sick, the fallen, the sinful, exactly as he did when he sent his only-begotten Son into the world to die for mankind. God never changes his moods or cools off in his affections or loses his enthusiasm.[2]

So here is great comfort. If God varied as his creatures do, if he willed one thing today and another thing tomorrow, who could confide in him or be encouraged by him? No one. But God is always the same. We shall always find him as he has disclosed himself to be in Christ Jesus. The one who has this assurance will not fail to come to him in times of trouble.

What God Intends; What God Says

God is also immutable in his purposes or plans. We often change plans. Usually we have lacked foresight to anticipate everything that might happen, or we have lacked power to execute what we purposed. God is not like us in that respect. "Infinite in wisdom, there can be no error in [his plans'] conception; infinite in power, there can be no failure in their accomplishment."[3]

"God is not man, that he should lie, or a son of man, that he should repent. Has he said, and will he not do it? Or has he spoken, and will he not fulfil it?" (Num. 23:19). Repenting means to revise one's plan of action, but God never does so. His plans are made on the basis of perfect knowledge, and his perfect power sees to their accomplishment. "The counsel of the LORD stands for ever, the thoughts of his heart to all generations" (Ps. 33:11); "The LORD of hosts has sworn: 'As I have planned, so shall it be, and as I have purposed, so shall it stand' " (Is. 14:24). "Remember the former things of old; for I am God, and there is no other; I am God, and there is none like me, declaring the end from the beginning and from ancient times things not yet done, saying, 'My counsel shall stand, and I will accomplish all my purpose' " (Is. 46:9-10). Solomon wrote, "Many are the plans in the mind of a man, but it is the purpose of the LORD that will be established" (Prov. 19:21).

What are the consequences of God's immutability? First, if God's purposes do not change, then *God's purposes for Christ will not change*. His purpose is to glorify him. "Therefore God has highly exalted him and bestowed on him the name which is above every name, that at the name of Jesus every knee should bow, in heaven and on earth and under the earth, and every tongue confess that Jesus Christ is Lord, to the glory of God the Father" (Phil. 2:9-11).

It is foolish then to resist Christ's glory. We may do so now, as many do, but the day is coming when Jesus must be confessed as Lord even by those who would not have him as Lord in this life. In these verses the word that is translated *confess (exomologeo)* more often means "to acknowledge" than it means "to confess with thanksgiving." For example, it is used of an acknowledgement or confession of sin or of Judas's agreeing with the chief priests to betray his master. It is in the sense of acknowledgement that the word is used of those who have rebelled against Christ's authority and glory in this life. They have rejected him here, but they will acknowledge him there. They will not confess that "Jesus Christ is Lord" with gladness, but they will confess it as they are banished from his presence forever.

Second, *God's purposes for his redeemed people will not change.* He intends to make them into the image of Jesus Christ (as we saw in chapter thirteen) and to bring them safely into his presence at the end of their earthly pilgrimage. In the Epistle to the Hebrews God's promises to Abraham are said to disclose the nature of his promises to us.

> *For when God made a promise to Abraham, since he had no one greater by whom to swear, he swore by himself, saying, "Surely I will bless you and multiply you." And thus Abraham, having patiently endured, obtained the promise. Men indeed swear by a greater than themselves, and in all their disputes an oath is final for confirmation. So when God desired to show more convincingly to the heirs of the promise the unchangeable character of his purpose, he interposed with an oath, so that through two unchangeable things, in which it is impossible that God should prove false, we who have fled for refuge might have strong encouragement to seize the hope set before us. (Heb. 6:13-19)*

God's purpose is to bring his own into full enjoyment of their promised inheritance, into their hope. So they can know it and be assured of it, he confirms it by an immutable oath. In that purpose every redeemed child of God should take courage.

Finally, *God's purposes for the wicked will not change.* It is his purpose to judge them, and that he will do. God "will by no means clear the guilty" (Ex. 34:7). Many other passages speak, often in vivid terms, of the judgment itself. The immutability of God's judgments should be a warning to any who have not yet turned to the Lord Jesus Christ as Savior and should impel them toward him while there is yet hope.

The unchangeableness of God also means that God's truth does not change.

Men sometimes say things that they do not really mean, simply because they do not know their own mind; also, because their views change, they frequently find that they can no longer stand to things that they said in the past. All of us sometimes have to recall our words, because hard facts refute them. The words of men are unstable things. But not so the words of God. They stand forever, as abidingly valid expressions of his mind and thought. No circumstances prompt him to recall them; no changes in his own thinking require him to amend them. Isaiah writes, "All flesh is grass . . . the grass withereth . . . but the word of our God shall stand for ever" (Is. 40:6-8).[4]

Christians should stand on the word and promises of our immutable God. God's promises are not "relics of a bygone age," as Packer notes, but rather the eternally valid disclosure of the mind and will of our heavenly Father. His promises will not alter. A wise man or woman builds on this truth.

PART IV
GOD'S CREATION

Then God said, "Let us make man in our image, after our likeness; and let them have dominion over the fish of the sea, and over the birds of the air, and over the cattle, and over all the earth, and over every creeping thing that creeps upon the earth." So God created man in his own image, in the image of God he created him; male and female he created them. (Gen. 1:26-27)

In the beginning God created the heavens and the earth. (Gen. 1:1)

Then I looked, and I heard around the throne and the living creatures and the elders the voice of many angels, numbering myriads of myriads and thousands of thousands, saying with a loud voice, "Worthy is the Lamb who was slain, to receive power and wealth and wisdom and might and honor and glory and blessing!" (Rev. 5:11-12)

Many are the plans in the mind of a man, but it is the purpose of the LORD that will be established. (Prov. 19:21)

15

THE
CREATION
OF MAN

There are three reasons why the creation of man must be studied when dealing with the knowledge of God: one general, one specific and one theological. The general reason is that creation as a whole reveals something of its Creator so that, as was seen in chapter two, even though a man or woman will not worship and serve God, nevertheless what is revealed about God in nature will rise up to confound and condemn that person. The specific reason is that man as a unique part of that creation is made in the image of God, according to the Bible's testimony. Mankind reveals aspects of God's being that are not seen in the rest of the created order but must be seen if we are to understand God. The theological reason is that since we cannot have a genuine knowledge of God unless it is accompanied by a corresponding knowledge of ourselves, we must at least know ourselves—made in God's image, fallen and yet redeemed—if we would truly know and reverence our Creator.

The place to begin in a study of God's creation is with humankind in general, for men and women are the most important part of creation. To say that humanity is the most important part of creation might be thought to be a provincial or chauvinistic statement (that is, as if we were fish, we would undoubtedly say that fish were most important). But men and women actually are, and sense themselves to be, higher than forms of the creation around them. They rule over creation, for one thing, and not by brute force either, for many animals are stronger. Rather they rule by the power of their minds and personality. For another thing, men and women have "God-consciousness," which animals don't have. God-consciousness causes them to become guilty in God's sight for refusing to worship him. No animal is guilty of moral or spiritual sin. On the other hand, God-consciousness is also our glory. For no other creature can in the same sense truly "glorify God, and enjoy him forever."

The Bible stresses our high position when it says toward the end of the first creation account: "Then God said, 'Let us make man in our image, after our likeness; and let them have dominion over the fish of the sea, and over the birds of the air, and over the cattle, and over all the earth, and over every creeping thing that creeps upon the earth.' So God created man in his own image, in the image of God he created him; male and female he created them" (Gen. 1:26-27).

In these verses our uniqueness and superiority to the rest of creation are expressed in three ways. First, we are said to have been made "in God's image," which is not said of either objects or animals. Second, we are given dominion over the fish, birds, animals and even the earth itself. Third, there is a repetition of the word *created*. The same word is used at only three points in the creation narrative: first, when God created matter from nothing (v. 1); second, when God created conscious life (v. 21); and third, when God created mankind (v. 27). The progression is from the body (or matter) to soul (or personality) to spirit (or life with God-consciousness). Thus, humanity stands at the pinnacle of creation. As Francis Schaeffer writes, by repeating the word *created,* "it is as though God put exclamation points here to indicate that there is something special about the creation of man."[1]

In God's Image

Let's look more closely at what it means to be created in the image of God. One thing it means is that women and men possess those attributes of *personality* that God himself possesses, but that animals, plants and matter do not. To have personality one must possess knowledge, feelings (including religious feelings) and a will. God has personality, and so do we. To say that an animal possesses something akin to human personality is meaningful only to a point. Personality, in the sense that we are speaking of it here, is something that links humanity to God but does not link either humanity or God to the rest of creation.

A second element in being created in the image of God is *morality.* Morality includes the two further elements of freedom and responsibility. To be sure, the freedom which men and women possess is not absolute. Even in the beginning the first man, Adam, and the first woman, Eve, were not autonomous. They were creatures and were responsible for acknowledging their status by their obedience. Since the Fall that freedom has been further restricted so that, as Augustine said, the original *posse non peccare* ("able not to sin") has become a *non posse non peccare* ("not able not to sin"). Still there is a limited freedom for women and men even in their fallen state, and with that comes moral responsibility. In brief, we do not need to sin always as we do, or as often as we do. And even when we sin under compulsion (as may sometimes be the case), we still know that it is wrong—and thus we inadvertently confess our likeness to God (though fallen) in morality as in other areas.

The third element in being made in God's image is *spirituality.* Humanity exists for communion with God who is Spirit

(Jn. 4:24). This communion is intended to be eternal as God is eternal. Here we might say that although we have physical bodies, as do plants, and souls, as do animals, only human beings possess spirits. It is on the level of the spirit alone that we are aware of God and commune with him.

There is an ongoing debate between those who believe in a three-part construction of our being and those who believe that man can properly be considered on two levels only. The debate need not overly concern us. All parties to the debate recognize that human beings consist at least of the physical part that dies and needs to be resurrected and of an immaterial part that lives beyond death, the part we call the person himself. The only question is whether the immaterial part can be further distinguished as containing that which men and women share with animals—personality in the limited sense—and spirit, which relates them to God.

Here the linguistic data should be determinative, but they are not as clear as one could wish. Sometimes, particularly in the earlier parts of the Old Testament, soul *(nephesh)* and spirit *(ruach)* are used interchangeably, which has introduced confusion. Still, as time went on, *ruach* increasingly came to designate that element by which men and women relate to God, in distinction from *nephesh* which then meant merely the life-principle. In conformity to that distinction, "soul" is often used in reference to animals, but "spirit" is not. Conversely, the prophets, who heard the voice of God and communed with him in a special sense, are always said to be animated by the "spirit" (but not the "soul") of God. In the New Testament the linguistic data are similar. Thus, while soul *(psyche)* and spirit *(pneuma)* are sometimes freely exchanged for one another as in the Old Testament, *pneuma* nevertheless also expresses that particular capacity for relating to God which is the redeemed person's glory, as opposed to *psyche* which even the unsaved and unresponsive possess (1 Cor. 2:9-16). It is possible, though not certain, that in the

Pauline writings the spirit of a man or woman is considered as being lost or dead as a result of the Fall and as being restored only in those who are regenerate.[2]

Yet we must not get off the track here. For whether we speak of two parts or three parts to man's being, an individual is nevertheless a unity. His or her salvation consists in the redemption of the whole, not merely of the soul or spirit, just as (in a parallel but contrary way) each part is affected by sin.

In this area the particular words used are less important than the truths they are meant to convey. Even those who would insist most strongly on the unity of man nevertheless believe that he is more than matter. Or, if they adhere to a two-part scheme, they nevertheless recognize that there is something about man that sets him off from animals. That is all that the distinction between spirit and soul in the three-part system means. Spirit, soul and body are simply good terms to use to talk about what it really means to be a human being.

The *body*, then, is the part of the person we see, the part that possesses physical life. At first glance we tend to think that this is what differentiates us from God, and it does in a sense. We have a body; he does not. But upon further consideration this distinction is not so obvious as it might seem. What about the Incarnation of the Lord Jesus Christ, for instance? Or again, which came first in the mind of God, the body of Christ or Adam's body? Did Christ become like us by means of the Incarnation or did we become like him by means of God's creative act? Calvin, who discusses this question briefly in the *Institutes,* does not believe that Adam was fashioned on the pattern of the Messiah to come. Calvin dismisses the idea that Christ would have come even if Adam had not sinned.[3] But the two ideas are not necessarily in conflict. One might even speculate that when God walked in the garden with Adam and Eve before the Fall, he did so as the second person of the Trinity, in a preincarnate but nevertheless corporeal form.

The point of the discussion is that our bodies are of great

value and should be honored in the way we treat them. As redeemed men and women, we should see that our bodies are God's "temples" (1 Cor. 6:19).

The soul is the part of man that we call "personality." It is also not a simple matter to talk about. The soul is certainly related to the body through the brain, and is a part of the body. It is also difficult to think of it without the qualities we associate with spirit. Nevertheless, in general terms, soul refers at least to what makes the individual a unique individual. We might say that the soul centers in the mind and includes all likes and dislikes, special abilities or weaknesses, emotions, aspirations and anything else that makes the individual different from all others of his species. Because we have souls we are able to have fellowship, love and communication with one another.

But we do not have fellowship, love and communication only with others of our species. We also have love and communion with God, for which we need a *spirit*. The spirit is, therefore, that part of human nature that communes with God and partakes in some measure of God's own essence. God is nowhere said to be body or soul, though he may possess each of these aspects in the senses indicated earlier. But God *is* defined as spirit. "God is spirit," said Jesus. Therefore, "Those who worship him must worship in spirit and truth" (Jn. 4:24). Because man is spirit (or comes to possess a spirit once more by means of new birth), he can have fellowship with God and love him.

Herein lies our true worth. We are made in God's image and are therefore valuable to God and to others. God loves men and women, far beyond his love for animals, plants or inanimate matter. Moreover, he feels for men and women, identifies with them in Christ, grieves for them and intervenes in history to make each of us into all he has determined we should be. We get some idea of the special nature of this relationship when we remember that in a similar way the woman, Eve, was made in the image of man. Therefore, though different, Adam saw himself in her and loved her as his companion and corresponding member in the universe. It is not wrong to say that men and women are to God somewhat as a woman is to a man. They are God's unique and valued companions. In support of this idea we need only to think of the New Testament teaching concerning Christ as the bridegroom and the church as his bride.

Moral Agents

Another part of being made in the image of God is that we are responsible moral agents in God's universe. Moral responsibility is implied in the attributes of our being (knowledge, feelings, will, God-consciousness) and in the test of obedience to God given later (Gen. 2:16-17). Yet the concept is present even in the creation account. The same verse that tells of God's decision to make man in his own image also tells us that he is to "have dominion over the fish of the sea, and over the birds of the air, and over the cattle, and over all the earth, and over every creeping thing that creeps upon the earth" (Gen. 1:26). Dominion of any kind, but particularly of this scope, clearly involves the ability to act responsibly.

Today in the Western world there is a strong tendency to deny human moral responsibility on the basis of some kind of determinism. The Bible does not allow such a possibility. Today's determinism usually takes one of two forms. It may be a physical, mechanical determinism ("human beings are the product of their genes and body chemistry") or it may be a psychological determinism ("human beings are the product of their environment and past history"). In either case the individual is excused from responsibility for what he or she does. Thus, we have gone through a period in which criminal behavior was increasingly termed a sickness, and the criminal was regarded more as a victim of his environment than as the victimizer. (Recently there has been a tendency at least to reconsider this matter.) Less blatant but nevertheless morally reprehensible acts are still excused with statements like "I suppose he just couldn't help it."

The biblical view could hardly be more different. Schaeffer notes, "Since God has made man in his own image, man is not caught in the wheels of determinism. Rather man is so great that he can influence history for himself and for others, for this life and the life to come."[4] We are fallen, but even in our fallen state we are responsible. We can do great things, or we can do terrible things, things for which we must give an accounting before God.

There are four areas in which our responsibility should be exercised. First, it should be exercised *toward God*. God is the One who created man and woman and gave them dominion over the created order. Consequently, they were responsible to him for what they did with it. When man sins, as the Genesis account goes on to show he does, it is God who comes to require a reckoning: "Where are you? . . . Who told you that you were naked? . . . What is this that you have done?" (Gen. 3:9, 11, 13). In the thousands of years since Eden, many have convinced themselves that they are responsible to no one. But the testimony of Scripture is that this area of responsibility still stands and that all will one day answer to God at the judgment of the great white throne. "And the dead were judged by what was written in the books, by what they had done" (Rev. 20:12).

Second, people are responsible for their acts *toward other people*. That is the reason for those biblical statements instituting capital punishment as a proper response to murder; for instance, "Whoever sheds the blood of man, by man shall his blood be shed" (Gen. 9:6). Such verses are not in the Bible as relics of a more barbarous age or because in the biblical outlook people are not valuable. Rather, they are there for the opposite reason. They are there because people are too valuable to be wantonly destroyed, and thus the harshest penalties are reserved for those who commit such destruction.

In a related way, James 3:9-10 forbids the use of the tongue in cursing others for the simple reason that all others are also made in God's image. "With it we bless the Lord and Father, and with it we curse men, who are made in the likeness of God. ... My brethren, this ought not to be so." In these texts murder of another or cursing of another is forbidden on the grounds that the other person (even after the Fall) retains something of God's image and is therefore to be valued by us, as God also values him.

Third, we have a responsibility _toward nature_ (to be discussed in more detail in the next chapter). We need to see that how we behave toward nature, whether we cultivate and advance it or whether we use and destroy it, is not without moral dimensions. Nor is it a matter of indifference to God. The depth of this responsibility is seen in the way in which God himself speaks of nature, noting that "the creation was subjected to futility" by reason of man's sin, but that it shall yet "be set free from its bondage to decay and obtain the glorious liberty of the children of God" at the time of the final resurrection and consummation of all things (Rom. 8:20-21).

The fourth area of an individual's responsibility is _toward himself or herself_. As the Bible describes them, the man and the woman were made "a little lower than the angels" (Ps. 8:5 KJV); that is, they were placed between the highest and lowest beings, between angels and beasts.[5] But it is significant that we are described as being slightly lower than the angels rather than being slightly higher than the beasts. Our place and privilege is to be a mediating figure, but to be one who looks up rather than down. When we sever the tie that binds us to God and try to cast off God's rule, we do not rise up to take God's place, as we desire to do, but rather sink to a more bestial level. In fact, we come to think of ourselves as beasts ("the naked ape") or, even worse, as machines.

In contrast, the redeemed man or woman (who has the God-tie restored) is to look up and exercise full responsibility toward himself or herself on each level of his or her being. We each have a body, and we must use it as what it really is, "the temple of God's spirit." We must not allow it to be corrupted by physical laziness, overeating, habit-forming drugs, alcohol or any other physically debilitating practice. We each have a soul, and we must use it fully—allowing our minds and personalities to develop as God blesses and instructs us. We each have a spirit, which we must exercise in worshiping and serving the true God.

Christians particularly need to use and develop their minds. Today there is a strong tendency toward a mindless or anti-intellectual form of Christianity, as John R. W. Stott points out in *Your Mind Matters.* This anti-intellectualism is unfortunate because it is through the mind that God primarily speaks to us (as we study his Word and think about it), causes us to grow in grace ("by the renewal of your mind," Rom. 12:2), and allows us to win others (by giving a "defense" for our Christian hope, 1 Pet. 3:15).

> *The current mood (cultivated in some Christian groups) of anti-intellectualism . . . is not true piety at all but part of the fashion of the world and therefore a form of worldliness. To denigrate the mind is to undermine foundational Christian doctrines. Has God created us rational beings, and shall we deny our humanity which he has given to us? Has God spoken to us, and shall we not listen to his words? Has God renewed our mind through Christ, and shall we not think with it? Is God going to judge us by his Word, and shall we not be wise and build our house upon this rock?* [6]

Clearly Christians should allow God to develop them intellectually to the fullest extent, thereby becoming known as thinking men and women. As Stott goes on to show, without respect for the mind there is no true worship, faith, holiness, guidance, evangelism or Christian ministry.

Shattered Image

In this chapter we have been looking at man as God made him

and intends him to be—that is, before the Fall or as he will eventually become in Christ. Nevertheless, it wouldn't be right to ignore the fact that, although men and women were made in the image of God, that image has nevertheless been greatly marred or shattered as a result of their sin. True, vestiges of the image remain. But we are today not what God intended. We are fallen beings, and the effects of the Fall are seen on each level of our being: body, soul and spirit.

When God gave Adam and Eve the test of the forbidden tree, which was to be a measure of their obedience and responsibility toward the One who had created them, God said, "You may freely eat of every tree of the garden; but of the tree of the knowledge of good and evil you shall not eat, for in the day that you eat of it you shall die" (Gen. 2:16-17). The woman was deceived by the serpent and ate. She came to Adam; Adam, who was not deceived, still ate and in a sense said to God, "I don't care about all the other trees you have given me; as long as this tree stands here in the midst of the garden it reminds me of my dependence on you and therefore I hate it; I will eat its fruit regardless of the consequences." So he did eat of it and he did die. His spirit, that part of him that had communion with God, died instantly. His spiritual death is clear from the fact that he ran from God when God came to him in the garden. Men and women have been running and hiding ever since. Further, the soul, the seat of intellect, feelings and identity, began to die. So men and women began to lose a sense of their own identity, to give vent to bad feelings and to suffer the decay of their intellect. Describing this type of decay, Paul says that, having rejected God, people inevitably "became futile in their thinking and their senseless minds were darkened. Claiming to be wise, they became fools, and exchanged the glory of the immortal God for images resembling mortal man or birds or animals or reptiles" (Rom. 1:21-23). Eventually even the body dies. So it is said of us all, "You are dust, and to dust you shall return" (Gen. 3:19).

Donald Grey Barnhouse has compared the result to a three-story house that has been bombed in wartime and severely damaged. The bomb has destroyed the top floor entirely. Debris has fallen down into the second floor, severely damaging it. The weight of the two ruined floors plus the shock have produced cracks in the walls of the first floor so that it is doomed to collapse eventually. Thus it was with Adam. His body was the dwelling of the soul and his spirit was above that. When he fell, the spirit was entirely destroyed, the soul ruined and the body destined to final collapse and ruin.[7]

However, the glory and fullness of the Christian gospel are seen at precisely this point. For when God saves an individual he saves the whole person, beginning with the spirit, continuing with the soul and finishing with the body. The salvation of the spirit comes first; God first establishes contact with the one who has rebelled against him. That is regeneration or the new birth. Second, God begins to work with the soul, renewing it after the image of the perfect man, the Lord Jesus Christ. That work is sanctification. Finally, there is the resurrection in which even the body is redeemed from destruction.

Moreover, God makes of the redeemed person a new creation as Paul suggests in 2 Corinthians 5:17. He does not merely patch up the old spirit, the old soul and the old body, as if the collapsing house were just being buttressed up and given a new coat of paint. Rather he creates a new spirit which is his own Spirit within the individual, a new soul (known as the new man) and a new body. That body is on the same order as the resurrection body of the Lord Jesus Christ. Today we are saved as Christians, but we are also in the process of salvation which means that the present matters. Moreover, we have an eye on the future, for it is only at the future moment of the resurrection that the redemption begun in this life will be complete and we will stand perfected before our great God and Savior, even Jesus Christ.

16   NATURE

It isn't enough to study human nature to learn about God through creation, for humanity does not make up the whole of the created order. Nor, for that matter, is it first, except in importance. Actually, the man and woman were the last of God's creation, having been made on the last of the six days. When the man and woman were created there already was a beautiful and varied universe established by God to receive them. So we conclude that nature should be studied, if for no other reasons than because it is there, was there first and is our inescapable environment.

But there are more important reasons. For one thing, nature too reveals God, even by itself. It is a limited revelation, as has been pointed out several times already. But it is still a revelation, and it becomes a fuller revelation for those who are redeemed. This thought is the basis of the nineteenth psalm. "The heavens are telling the glory of God; and the firmament proclaims his handiwork" (v. 1). Further, men and women are not only in nature in the sense of nature being their environment. They are linked to nature as also being finite and created. True, there is a distinction between humanity and the rest of nature. Men and women alone are made in the image of God. But the purposes of God on a human level will therefore unfold fully only when God's purposes with nature are also included in the picture.

A Major Question

The big question in reference to nature is: Where did the universe come from? Something is there—an immense, intricate and orderly something. It was there before we were. We cannot even imagine our existence without it. But how did it get there? And how did it get to be as we detect it?

As with all big questions, only a few answers are possible. One view is that the universe had no origin. That is, there is no origin to the universe because in some form the universe always existed; matter existed. Second, everything came from a personal something and that personal something was good (which corresponds to the Christian view). Third, everything came from a personal something and that something was bad. Fourth, there is and always has been a dualism. The last view takes several forms, depending on whether one is thinking of a personal or impersonal, moral or amoral dualism, but the views are related.

The four possibilities may be narrowed down. Number three, which gives a personal but evil origin to the universe, doesn't need to be pursued at great length, for, although it is a philosophical possibility, hardly anybody seriously upholds it. While it is possible to think of evil as a corruption of the good, it is not really possible to think of good as having emerged out of evil. Evil can be a misuse of otherwise good traits or abilities. But there is nothing for the good to come from if only evil exists.

The fourth possibility is unsatisfying too although its deficiencies are not readily apparent. Belief in a dualism has often been popular and has endured for long periods of history, but it does not stand up under close analysis. For, having stated a dualism, we immediately want to pass behind it to some type of unity that includes the dualism. Or else we choose one part of the dualism and make it prominent over the other, in which case we are really easing into one of the other possibilities.

C. S. Lewis has pointed to the catch in this system. According to dualism, the two powers (spirits or gods), one good and one evil, are supposed to be independent and eternal. Neither is responsible for the other, and each has an equal right to call itself God. Each presumably thinks that it is good and the other bad. But what do we mean when we say that the one power is good and the other bad? Do we mean merely that we prefer the one to the other? If that is all we mean, then we must give up any real talk about good or evil. And if we do that, then the moral dimension of the universe vanishes entirely, and we are left with nothing more than matter operating in certain ways. We cannot mean that and still hold to the dualism.

If, on the contrary, we mean that one power really is good and the other really is bad, then we are actually introducing some third thing into the universe, "some law or standard or rule of good which one of the powers conforms to and the other fails to conform to." And this standard, rather than the others, will turn out to be God. Lewis concludes, "Since the two powers are judged by this standard, then this standard, or the Being who made this standard, is farther back and higher up than either of them, and he will be the real God. In fact, what we meant by calling them good and bad turns out to be that one of them is in a right relation to the real ultimate God and the other in a wrong relation to him."[1]

Again, we may say that for the evil power to be evil he must possess the attributes of intelligence and will. But since these attributes are in themselves good, he must be getting them from the good power and is thus dependent upon him.

Neither an evil origin for the universe, from which good arose, nor a dualism adequately accounts for reality as we know it. So the real alternative is between the view which posits an eternity of matter and the view which sees everything as having come into existence through the will of an eternal, personal and moral God.

The first view is the dominant philosophy of current Western civilization. That view usually does not deny that there is such a thing as personality in the world today, but it conceives of it as having arisen out of impersonal substance. It does not deny the complexity of the universe, but it supposes that the complexity came from what was less complex and that in turn from something still less complex until eventually one arrives back at what is ultimately simple, that is, to matter. Matter, it is supposed, always existed—because there is no further explanation. That view is the philosophical basis of most modern science and it is what lies beneath most ideas of evolution.

But such a description of the origin of the universe has already introduced problems which the theory itself apparently has no means of solving. First, we have spoken of a form to matter and then of more complex forms. But where does form come from? Form means organization and perhaps purpose. But how can organization and purpose come from matter? Some would insist that organization and purpose were in the matter inherently, like genes in an egg or spermatozoon. But in addition to making nonsense of the theory—such matter is no longer *mere* matter—the basic question still remains unanswered, for the problem is how the organization and purpose got there. At some level, then, either early or late, we have to account for the form; we soon find ourselves looking for the Former, Organizer or Purposer.

Moreover, we also have introduced the idea of the personal; if we begin with an impersonal universe, we have no real explanation for the emergence of personality. Francis

and other biblical evidence suggest the three members of
Trinity being present at the beginning, having existed
ore anything else. The elements that we associate with the
nity—love, personality and communication—are there-
e eternal and have value. This is the Christian answer to
human fear of being lost in an impersonal and loveless
verse.

he second major point of Genesis 1 is that the creation was
ording to *an orderly unfolding of the mind and purposes of God.*
at is, it was a step-by-step progression, marked by a se-
nce of six significant days. We read this account, and im-
diately we think of questions along a scientific line that we
uld like to have answered: Is the sequence of the Genesis
s to be compared with the sequence of the so-called geo-
ical periods? Do the fossils substantiate this narrative? How
g are the "days"—twenty-four-hour periods or indefinite
s? And, perhaps most important, does the Genesis account
ve room for evolutionary development (guided by God) or
s it require a divine intervention and instantaneous crea-
n in each case? The chapter doesn't answer our questions.
ted a moment ago that the Genesis account is a theological
her than a scientific statement, and we need to keep that in
id here. It is true that it provides us with grounds for con-
active speculation, and at some points it is even rather exit. But it isn't written primarily to answer such questions;
must remember that.

ctually, there is no firm biblical reason for rejecting some
ms of evolutionary theory, so long as it is carefully qual-
d at key points. There is, for example, no reason to deny
t one form of fish may have evolved from another form or
n that one form of land animal may have evolved from a
creature. The Hebrew term translated by our word *let,*
ich occurs throughout the creation account, would permit
h a possibility.

here are, however, three significant points at which a

Schaeffer writes, "The assumption of an imp
ning can never adequately explain the perso
see around us, and when men try to explain m
of an original impersonal, man soon disappe

Christianity begins with the remaining answe
maintains that the universe exists with form a
as we know it does, because it has been brought
personal and orderly God. In other words, Go
fore the universe came into existence, and he
sonal. He created all we know, including ou
quently, the universe quite naturally bears th

In the Beginning

What do we find when we turn to the open
Genesis? Here the Christian view is stated fo
and in definitive form. It is a theological staten
and we must acknowledge this because if we d
evitably find ourselves looking for a scientific
things and will be misled. Not that the Genesi
opposed to any established scientific data; tru
if it really is truth, will never contradict truth ir
Still Genesis 1 is not a description from which
to find answers to purely scientific questions.
statement of origins in the area of meanings, p
relationship of all things to God.

The chapter makes three main points. Firs
vious, it teaches that *God stands at the beginning* o
is himself the One through whom all things c
tence. The chapter captures this eloquently in
words: "In the beginning God . . ." At the ve
then, our thought is directed to the existence
this God.

In the Hebrew language the name for God
Elohim, a plural form. That it is plural suggests
plural dimensions to his being. In chapter ten I

unique action of God to create in a special sense seems to be marked off by the powerful Hebrew word *bara,* rendered "created." *Bara* generally means to create out of nothing, which means that the activity it describes is therefore a prerogative of God. And, as I pointed out in chapter fifteen, it is used in Genesis 1 to mark the creation of matter, of personality and of God-consciousness. This means that although there may have been something like an evolutionary development taking place in the periods between the use of the word *bara,* this was not the case at least at those three points. Besides, the chapter teaches that the whole creation was not a random development but rather a result of the direct guidance of God.

It should be noted that today's scientific world may be witnessing the beginnings of a movement away from some forms of naturalistic evolution, particularly Darwinism, as an explanation of the universe. To give one example, the February 1976 issue of *Harper's Magazine* carried an important article by Thomas Bethell, editor of *The Washington Monthly,* entitled "Darwin's Mistake." It was essentially a review of recent writing on the evolution question, and its point was that scientists are in the process of quietly abandoning Darwin's theory. Why? Because, according to Bethell, Darwin's theory fails to account for the very thing that evolution is supposed to account for, namely, the varieties of plants, fish, animals and other forms of life.

In Darwin's approach the key element was natural selection, which was supposed to explain how the various forms came about. But as scientists look back on his theory, they see natural selection as explaining only how some organisms had more offspring than others and therefore survived, but not how there came to be the various organisms (some of which survived and some of which did not survive) in the first place. Bethell observes, "There is, then, no 'selection' by nature at all. Nor does nature 'act,' as it is so often said to do in biology books. One organism may indeed be 'fitter' than another from an evolutionary point of view, but the only event that determines this fitness is death (or infertility). This, of course, is not something which helps *create* the organism, but is something that terminates it."

The author concludes, "Darwin, I suggest, is in the process of being discarded, but perhaps in deference to the venerable old gentleman, resting comfortably in Westminster Abbey next to Sir Isaac Newton, it is being done as discreetly and gently as possible, with a minimum of publicity."[3]

The third point of the Genesis account of creation is *God's moral pronouncement* upon what he has done. It appears in the repeated phrase, "And God saw that it was good." This pronouncement is not made in reference to some object because we in a pragmatic way can point to it and say, "That thing is useful to me." God's pronouncement upon the goodness of the rest of creation came before we were even made. And that means that a tree, to give an example, is not good only because we can cut it down and make a house out of it or because we can burn it in order to get heat. It is good because God made it and pronounced it good. It is good because, like everything else in creation, it conforms to God's nature. Schaeffer writes of the divine benediction, "This is not a relative judgment, but a judgment of the holy God who has a character and whose character is the law of the universe. His conclusion: Every step and every sphere of creation, and the whole thing put together—man himself and his total environment, the heavens and the earth—conforms to myself."[4]

God's evaluation in Genesis 1 is confirmed by God's covenant with the human race and the earth given at the time of Noah—after the Fall. There God says, "Behold, I establish my covenant with you and your descendants after you, and with every living creature that is with you, the birds, the cattle, and every beast of the earth with you, as many as came out of the ark.... I set my bow in the cloud, and it shall be a sign of the covenant between me and the earth" (Gen. 9:9-10, 13).

Here God's concern is expressed, not just for Noah and those human beings who were with him in the ark, but for the birds and cattle and even the earth itself. His whole creation is "good."

Similarly, Romans 8 expresses the value of all God has made. He intends to redeem the whole earth afflicted by the Fall. "The creation itself will be set free from its bondage to decay and obtain the glorious liberty of the children of God. We know that the whole creation has been groaning in travail together until now; and not only the creation, but we ourselves, who have the first fruits of the Spirit, groan inwardly as we wait for adoption as sons, the redemption of our bodies" (Rom. 8:21-23).

Response to Nature

The value of creation brings us to a natural conclusion: if God finds the universe good in its parts and as a whole, then we must find it good also. That doesn't mean that we will refuse to see that nature has been marred by sin. Indeed, the verses from Genesis 9 and Romans 8 are inexplicable apart from the realization that nature has suffered as a result of the Fall of mankind. It is marred by thorns, weeds, disease and death. But even in its marred state it has value, just as fallen humanity has value.

Therefore we must be *thankful* for the world God has made and praise him for it. In some expressions of Christian thought and piety, only the soul has value. That view is neither correct nor Christian. Actually, the elevation of the value of the soul and the debasement of the body and other material things is a pagan, Greek idea based on a false understanding of creation. If God had made the soul (or spirit) alone and if the material world had come from some lesser or even evil source, then the Greeks would have been right. But the Christian view is that God has made all that is and that it therefore has value and should be valued by us because of its origin.

Second, we should *delight* in creation. To delight is closely related to being thankful, but it is a step beyond it. It is a step that many Christians have never taken. Frequently Christians look on nature only as one of the classic proofs of God's existence. Instead, they should really enjoy what they see. We should appreciate natural beauty. Moreover, we should exult in it more than non-Christians because of its revelation of the God who stands behind nature.

Third, Christians should demonstrate a *responsibility* toward nature. We should not destroy it simply for the sake of destroying it but rather seek to elevate it to its fullest potential. There is a parallel here between the responsibility of men and women toward the creation and the responsibility of a husband toward his wife in marriage. In each case the responsibility is based on a God-given dominion (though the two are not identical). "Husbands, love your wives, as Christ loved the church and gave himself up for her, that he might sanctify her, having cleansed her by the washing of water with the word, that the church might be presented before him in splendor, without spot or wrinkle or any such thing, that she might be holy and without blemish" (Eph. 5:25-27). In a similar way, men and women together should properly seek to sanctify and cleanse the earth in order that it might be more as God created it, in anticipation of its ultimate redemption.

Certainly the universe is to be used by people in a proper way. Where trees are abundant, some can be cut down to make wood for a home. But they shouldn't be cut down simply for the pleasure of cutting them down or because that is the easiest way to increase the value of the ground. In every area careful thought must be given to the value and purpose of each object, and there must be a Christian rather than a purely utilitarian approach to it.

Finally, after they have contemplated nature and come to value it, Christians should turn once again to the God who made it and sustains it moment by moment and should learn to *trust* him. God cares for nature, in spite of its abuse through our sins. But if he cares for nature, then we may trust him to care for each of us also. Such an argument occurs in the midst of Christ's Sermon on the Mount in which he draws our attention to God's care of the birds (animal life) and lilies (plant life) and then asks, "Are you not of more value than they? ... But if God so clothes the grass of the field, which today is alive and tomorrow is thrown into the oven, will he not much more clothe you, O men of little faith?" (Mt. 6:26, 30).

17 THE SPIRIT WORLD

Before men and women were created, God had already made a beautiful and varied universe to receive them, as we saw in the last chapter. But if Job 38:7 is to be taken as referring to angels, as there is every reason for it to be, then even before the creation of the material universe there was a vast world of spirit beings. We don't know when these were created. In fact we know very little about them at all. But we know that they existed before all we can see was created and that they exist today. As God said to Job, "Where were you when I laid the foundation of the earth? Tell me, if you have understanding. Who determined its measurements—surely you know! Or who stretched the line upon it? On what were its bases sunk, or who laid its cornerstone, when the morning stars sang together, and all the *sons of God* shouted for joy?" (Job 38: 4-7).

It is interesting in view of the Bible's testimony to the existence of spirits that the mythologies of ancient civilizations also claim their existence. Babylonian mythology portrayed the spirits as gods who brought messages from the world of the gods above to earth beneath. Greek and Roman mythology had gods and semigods visiting the earth. So it is with virtually all ancient civilizations. Critics of the Bible sometimes see its references to a spirit world as evidence that the Bible is also mythology, that is, as having no factual basis, at least in that area. But it is equally possible that the mythologies actually preserve a distorted memory of an early experience of the race. That possibility is enhanced, even for non-Christians, by the striking current renewal of interest in the spirit world.

Are there such beings? Do angels or demons really exist? Do they visit earth? The Bible gives us trustworthy answers to such questions. Though it is true that the Bible does not tell us all that we might like to know—much about the origin and function of the spirit world is shrouded in mystery—it does tell us what needs to be known and tells us truly.

Angels

Angels are mentioned over one hundred times in the Old Testament and more than one hundred sixty times in the New Testament. We are told that they are God's messengers—that is what the word *angel* means. They are immortal; that is, they do not die, though they have been created and therefore are not eternal. They exist in vast numbers. "Then I looked, and I heard around the throne and the living creatures and the elders the voice of many angels, numbering myriads of myriads and thousands of thousands" (Rev. 5:11). Angels possess the elements of personality; they render intelligent worship to God: "saying with a loud voice, 'Worthy is the Lamb who was slain, to receive power and wealth and wisdom and might and honor and glory and blessing!' " (Rev. 5:12).

Some of these qualities are also indicated by the terms used to refer to them in Scripture. They are called the "heavenly host," for example (Lk. 2:13). That suggests that as the troops of an emperor surround his person and serve him, so these beings serve God and make his glory visible. They are called "principalities," "powers," "dominions," "authorities," and "thrones" (Eph. 1:21; Col. 1:16) because they are those through whom God administers his authority in the world.

The Bible also reveals something of an angelic hierarchy; certain classes or orders of angels are mentioned. In the first class is the angel most mentioned in the Bible: Michael (the names of only two angels are recorded). He is described as being "the archangel," that is, the head of all the holy angels. His name means "he who is like God" (Dan. 10:21, 12:1; 1 Thess. 4:16; Jude 9; Rev. 12:7-10).

A second category contains those who are God's special messengers. The second angel mentioned by name, Gabriel, would be in this category, for he was entrusted with a special revelation for Daniel, the message to Zacharias about the birth of John the Baptist, and the announcement of the birth of Jesus to the virgin Mary (Dan. 8:16; 9:21; Lk. 1:18-19, 26-38).

A third category contains those angels called "cherubim." They are depicted as magnificent creatures who surround God's throne and defend his holiness from any contamination by sin (Gen. 3:24; Ex. 25:18, 20; Ezek. 1:1-18). God instructed that gold figures of these beings be placed upon the mercy seat of the ark of the covenant within the Holy of Holies of the Jewish tabernacle. The cherubim may be identical with the "seraphim" described by Isaiah in chapter 6 (vv. 2-7).

Finally, there are vast numbers of angelic hosts to whom no special names are given. They are described merely as the "elect angels" to distinguish them from those angels that sinned with Satan and so fell from their first estate (see 1 Tim. 5:21).

The grandeur and complexity of the angelic world are enough to pique us to study it. But in addition, such study enhances our sense of God's glory. Calvin observes, "If we desire to recognize God from his works, we ought by no means to overlook such an illustrious and noble example" as his angels.[1]

Ministry of Angels

The first and most obvious work of angels is the *worship and praise of God,* which we see at many places in the Bible. For example, Isaiah writes that the seraphim, who stood above the throne of Jehovah, called one "to another and said: 'Holy, holy, holy, is the LORD of hosts; the whole earth is full of his glory' " (Is. 6:3). Daniel describes the scene as involving even greater numbers. "As I looked, thrones were placed and one that was ancient of days took his seat; his raiment was white as snow, and the hair of his head like pure wool; his throne was fiery flames, its wheels were burning fire. A stream of fire issued and came forth from before him; a thousand thousands served him, and ten thousand times ten thousand stood before him" (Dan. 7:9-10). In Revelation the angels—described as the four living creatures, the four and twenty elders (who may be redeemed human beings), and the thousands upon thousands of spirit beings— "never cease to sing, 'Holy, holy, holy, is the Lord God Almighty, who was and is and is to come!' " (Rev. 4:8; see 5:9-12).

The fact that the angels worship God in such numbers should both humble us and encourage us in our worship. It should humble us because God would not be deprived of worship even if we should fail to honor him. Angels are doing that already. On the other hand, it should encourage us because our voices shall one day be joined to those of the great angelic choir (Rev. 7:9-12; 19:1-6).

Second, angels *serve God* as agents of his many works. We read that angels were present at creation (Job 38:7) and at the giving of the law; the law is said to have been given "by the disposition of angels" (Acts 7:53; see Gal. 3:19; Heb. 2:2 KJV). An angel was the vehicle of God's revelation to Daniel;

several were used to reveal future events to the apostle John (Dan. 10:10-15; Rev. 17:1; 21:9; 22:16). Gabriel announced the births of both John the Baptist and of Jesus Christ (Lk. 1: 11-38; 2:9-12; Mt. 1:19-23). Many more sang of the event in the presence of the shepherds (Lk. 2:13-14). Similarly, at the time of Christ's temptation angels were present to minister to him (Mt. 4:11), as well as in the garden of Gethsemane (Lk. 22: 43), at the Resurrection to announce Christ's victory over death to the women who had come to the tomb (Mt. 28:2-7) and at the Ascension (Acts 1:10-11). They will appear again in large numbers at Christ's Second Coming (Mt. 24:31; 25:31; 2 Thess. 1:7).

Third, angels are ministering spirits sent to _assist and defend God's people._ Thus, we read, first in reference to Christ but then also to ourselves as his people, "For he will give his angels charge of you to guard you in all your ways. On their hands they will bear you up, lest you dash your foot against a stone" (Ps. 91:11-12). And, "The angel of the LORD encamps around those who fear him, and delivers them" (Ps. 34:7).

From a practical standpoint, if Christian people thought more often of this angelic protection, they would be less fearful of circumstances and enemies. At the same time our forgetfulness is understandable, for generally angels are not visible to us.

We are like Elisha's servant at Dothan before his vision of God's hosts. Elisha had been revealing the counsels of Israel's enemy Ben-hadad of Syria, to Israel's king, and Ben-hadad had reacted by trying to capture Elisha. Thus, by night he had surrounded Dothan where Elisha and his servant were staying. He was present in full force when Elisha's servant went out of the city to draw water the next morning. The account says that the servant discovered an "army" encompassing the city, "with horses and chariots." He was terrified! He ran to Elisha saying, "Alas, my master! What shall we do?"

Elisha replied, "Fear not, for those who are with us are more than those who are with them." Then he prayed that the young man's eyes might be opened to see the Lord's angels. "So the LORD opened the eyes of the young man, and he saw; and behold, the mountain was full of horses and chariots of fire round about Elisha" (2 Kings 6:15-17). Angels then struck the hosts of Ben-hadad with blindness so that Elisha was able to lead them captive into the Israelite capital of Samaria.

In a similar way we read that one angel of God killed one hundred eighty-five thousand soldiers of Assyria in order to deliver Jerusalem from Sennacherib's armies in the days of King Hezekiah.

A fourth special ministry of angels is in *service to God's people at the time of their death.* There are not many texts from which to argue this point, but it should be noticed that, according to Jesus, angels carried Lazarus to Abraham's bosom (Lk. 16:22).

Finally, angels are to be God's *agents in the final judgments* prophesied for men and women, the devils and this world. The extent of these judgments is more fully described in the book of Revelation than anywhere else. There is, first, a series of partial judgments against the earth released through the seals that are broken (Rev. 6:1—8:1), the trumpets that are blown (Rev. 8:2—11:19) and the seven bowls of wrath that are poured out (Rev. 15:1—16:21). These judgments fill the main part of the book and angels are associated with each one. Second, there is a judgment against the great city of Babylon (perhaps a symbol of Rome) and of those associated with her in her sins. Angels are also part of that judgment (Rev. 17:1—18:24). Third, there are judgments against the beast, who is probably antichrist, and against Satan and the false prophet (Rev. 19:17—20:3, 10). At last, there is the judgment of the great white throne at which the dead are judged according to their works (Rev. 20:11-15).

Fallen Angels
Mention of judgment, including the judgment against Satan,

leads to a second aspect of this subject. According to the Bible, there are legions of fallen angels who, under the malevolent rule of Satan, are bent on opposing God's rule and doing his people harm. They comprise a great and terrifying force, as the Bible describes them. But they are described for us not to induce terror but to warn us of danger so that we might draw near to God as the One who alone can protect us. The number of fallen angels can be gauged somewhat from the fact that Mary Magdalene alone is said to have been delivered from seven of them (Mk. 16:9; Lk. 8:2) and from knowing that many, calling themselves Legion, had possessed the man Christ encountered in the territory of the Gerasenes opposite Galilee (Lk. 8:26-33).

What is God's purpose in telling us of this vast host?

We have been forewarned that an enemy relentlessly threatens us, an enemy who is the very embodiment of rash boldness, of military prowess, of crafty wiles, of untiring zeal and haste, of every conceivable weapon and of skill in the science of warfare. We must, then, bend our every effort to this goal: that we should not let ourselves be overwhelmed by carelessness or faintheartedness, but on the contrary, with courage rekindled stand our ground in combat. [2]

The place to begin in preparing to stand against Satan and his hosts is with a knowledge of Satan himself, in both his strengths and weaknesses. And the place to begin knowing about Satan is with the fact that he is both real and personal. He is real in that he is not a figment of the human imagination. He is personal in that he is not merely some vague embodiment of evil. Jesus bore witness to these truths when he referred to the devil by name (Mt. 4:10; 16:23; Lk. 22:31) and when he overcame him at the time of his temptation in the wilderness (Mt. 4:1-11).

The idea of a personal devil has been denied by large segments of the Christian church and to some has become almost a laughing matter. Because of the revival of witchcraft and Satanism in recent years, it is perhaps not so much a laughing matter as before. Still, many would regard thoughts about the existence of a real devil as hardly serious. To the popular mind the devil is a funny creature in red underwear with horns and a tail. That is not at all the image of Satan portrayed in the Bible.

The apostle Paul noted that we are not ignorant of Satan's "devices" (2 Cor. 2:11 KJV). The word *device* means "a trick, plot, scheme, contrivance or stratagem." So the point is that Christians know, or should know, about Satan's tricks for seeking to blind people's minds and secure them for himself. One of these, which he uses at some points of history, is to make people believe that he does not exist.

The picture of a funny little being with horns has had an interesting development which at one point was connected (wrongly) with the Bible. In the Middle Ages, when most of the people were illiterate and the church used miracle plays to teach basic Bible stories, there was a need to make whatever character represented the devil immediately recognizable on the stage. The convention chosen was based on a pagan idea in vogue, according to which Satan was somewhat of a monster with horns. That caricature was assumed to be supported by the Bible.

In Isaiah, in a prophecy against Babylon, there is mention of a creature that would one day, it is said, roam about over the fallen and deserted city. The Hebrew word for this animal or creature is *sair*—meaning a wild goat—but few knew what it meant. So in some early translations of the Bible it was called a "satyr," which was one of the half-human, half-bestial figures of mythology. The Bible was thereby assumed to have described a creature like the then-popular Satan figure, and the medieval practice seemed vindicated. In modern times, with an equal lack of support, the devil has been conceived of as the sophisticated tempter of the Faust legend or of the popular American stage play and movie *Damn Yankees*.

Since the devil of fiction is so unbelievable, it is no wonder that millions discount him. But that is a mistake. According to Jesus, there is a devil and there are those who follow him. In fact, he warned his disciples to pray, "And lead us not into temptation, but deliver us from [the evil one]" (Mt. 6:13).

A Fallen Being

The devil exists and is a fallen being, as Jesus taught in John 8:44. Jesus showed the height from which Satan fell ("he has nothing to do with the truth") and the depths to which he descended ("he is a liar and the father of lies" and "he was a murderer from the beginning"). Jesus also said, "I saw Satan fall like lightning from heaven" (Lk. 10:18).

This point too is often rejected by men and women, even if they believe in a devil. Thus, rather than believing that Satan is a depraved form of what he once was, they prefer to think of him as heroic and, more or less, as the champion of fallen man. John Milton, though he did not glorify Satan, nevertheless contributed to that idea. Although it is true that in the opening pages of his great epic, _Paradise Lost_, Milton does describe the fall of Satan from heaven and later anticipates his final judgment, it is also true that the greater part of the first book of the epic describes Lucifer's heroic efforts to rise from the depths of hell and make something of his supposed new kingdom. Milton does this so brilliantly that it is possible to sympathize with Satan. We receive quite a different impression from Scripture.

To begin with, Satan has never been in hell and does not control hell. The Bible tells us that God has created hell, preparing it in part for the devil and his angels, and that Satan will one day end up there.

The Bible also describes Satan as at one time being "full of wisdom, and perfect in beauty." It says that he was once "in Eden, the garden of God," that he was "blameless" in all his ways from the day he was created, until "iniquity" was found in him (Ezek. 28:12-15).

In Isaiah we are told of Satan's fall through pride, which expressed itself in an arrogant desire to replace God. Satan says, "I will ascend to heaven; above the stars of God I will set my throne on high; I will sit on the mount of assembly in the far north; I will ascend above the heights of the clouds, I will make myself like the Most High." God replies that as a result of his sin he will actually be "brought down to Sheol, to the depths of the Pit" (Is. 14:13-15). This is not the portrait of a heroic being but of a fallen being. It is a being from whom a person should turn in horror.

Satan has wrought havoc on the human race. He is a murderer and the author of murder, as Jesus told his listeners. The first crime following the Fall of Adam and Eve was a murder; as a result of the Fall, Cain murdered his brother. We also read that Satan entered into Judas to betray Christ into the hands of his enemies so that they might kill him (Jn. 13:2). Satan's history is written in blood.

It is also written in deceit, for he is a liar, as Christ said. Satan lied to Eve—"You will not die" (Gen. 3:4). But she did die. In 1 Kings we read that lying spirits (presumably demons) went forth into the prophets of Ahab so that he would go into battle against the Syrians and fall at Ramoth-gilead (1 Kings 22:21-23). In Acts we are told that Satan entered into Ananias to cause him to lie about the price of his property, as a result of which he died (Acts 5:3). Satan lies today. Consequently we are to regard him as dangerous, deceitful and malicious, but above all as a sinner and as a failure. He sinned when he failed to remain in his high calling.

A Limited Being

Finally, Satan is a limited being. That is, he is not omniscient, as God is; he is not omnipotent, as God is; he is not omnipresent, as God is. If Satan is a murderer from the beginning, he is limited in the area of the ethical life. If he is to face judgment, he is obviously limited in power. Although we should be aware of Satan and warned about him, we should not get into the habit of thinking of the tempter as anything like an evil equivalent of God.

Satan is not omniscient. God knows all things but Satan does not. Above all, he doesn't know the future. No doubt Satan can make shrewd guesses, for he knows human nature and the tendencies of history. The so-called revelations of mediums and fortunetellers—when they aren't outright deceits —fall in this category. But they do not give true knowledge of what is to come. Thus, the predictions are vague and generally don't hold water. At one point God stated this in the form of a challenge to all false gods, saying, "Set forth your case, says the LORD; bring your proofs, says the King of Jacob. Let them bring them, and tell us what is to happen. . . . Tell us what is to come hereafter, that we may know that you are gods; do good, or do harm, that we may be dismayed and terrified. Behold, you are nothing, and your work is nought; an abomination is he who chooses you" (Is. 41:21-24).

Neither is Satan omnipotent. Thus, he cannot do everything he wants to do, and, in the case of believers especially, he can do only what God will permit. The best-known example is Job, who was safe until God had first lowered the hedge that he had thrown up about him. Even so God had his own worthwhile purposes and kept Job from sinning.

Satan is not omnipresent, which means that he cannot be everywhere at the same time tempting everybody. God is omnipresent. He can help all who call upon him, all at one time. But Satan must tempt one individual at a time or else operate through one or more of those angels, now demons, who fell with him. The interesting consequence of this fact is that Satan has probably never tempted you or anyone you know. Even in the Bible we find very few who were tempted by Satan directly. There was Eve, of course. Christ was tempted. Peter was tempted. The devil entered into Ananias to cause him to lie about the price of his land. But that is about all. On

one occasion Paul may have been hindered in his plans by
Satan (1 Thess. 2:18); but on another it was only a *messenger*
of Satan who bufféted him (2 Cor. 12:7). Similarly, lesser demons opposed an angel bringing a revelation to Daniel (Dan.
10:13, 20). And, although there may have been a great host of
devils that surrounded Elisha at Dothan—outnumbered by
the Lord's host, however—Satan himself is not said to have
been among them (2 Kings 6:16-17).

Although Christians must never ignore or underestimate
Satan and his stratagems, neither must they overestimate him.
Above all, they must never concentrate on Satan to the point
of taking their eyes away from God. God is our strength and
our tower. He limits Satan. God will never permit Christians to be tempted above what we are able to bear, and he will
always provide the way of escape that we may be able to bear
it (1 Cor. 10:13). As for Satan, his end is the lake of fire (Mt.
25:41).[3]

18 GOD'S PROVIDENCE

There is probably no point at which the Christian doctrine of God comes more into conflict with contemporary world views than in the matter of God's providence. Providence means that God has not abandoned the world that he created, but rather works within that creation to manage all things according to the "immutable counsel of His own will" (Westminister Confession of Faith, V, i). By contrast, the world at large, even if it will on occasion acknowledge God to have been the world's Creator, is at least certain that he does not now intervene in human affairs. Many think that miracles do not happen, that prayer isn't answered and that most things "fall out" according to the functioning of impersonal and unchangeable laws.

The world argues that evil abounds. How can evil be compatible with the concept of a good God who is actively ruling this world? There are natural disasters: fires, earthquakes, floods. In the past these have been called "acts of God." Should we blame God for them? Isn't it better to imagine that he simply has left the world to pursue its own course?

Such speculation can be answered on two levels. First, even from the secular perspective, such thinking is not as obvious as it seems. Second, it is not the teaching of the Bible.

A Universe on Its Own?

The idea of an absentee God is certainly not obvious in reference to nature, the first of the three major areas of God's creation discussed earlier. The great question about nature, raised by even the earliest Greek philosophers as well as by contemporary scientists, is why there is a pattern to nature's operations even though nature is constantly changing. Nothing is ever the same. Rivers flow, mountains rise and fall, flowers grow and die, the sea is in constant motion. Yet in a sense everything remains the same. The experience of one generation with nature is akin to the experience of generations that have gone before.

Science tends to explain this uniformity by the laws of averages or by laws of random motion. But that is not a full explanation. For example, by the very laws of averages it is quite possible that at some time all molecules of a gas or solid (or the great preponderance of them) might be moving in the same direction instead of in random directions, and if that were the case, then the substance would cease to be as we know it and the laws of science regarding it would be inoperable.

Where does uniformity come from if not from God? The Bible says that uniformity comes from God when it speaks of Christ "upholding the universe by his word of power" (Heb. 1:3) and argues that "in him all things hold together" (Col. 1:17). The point is that the providence of God lies behind the orderly world that we know. That was the primary thought in the minds of the authors of the Heidelberg Catechism when they defined *providence* as "the almighty and ever-present power of God whereby he still upholds, as it were by his own hand, heaven and earth together with all creatures, and rules in such a way that leaves and grass, rain and drought, fruitful and unfruitful years, food and drink, health and sickness, riches and poverty, and everything else, come to us not by chance but by his fatherly hand" (Question 27). Remove the providence of God over nature, and—not only is all sense of security gone—the world is gone; meaningless change would soon replace its order.

The same thing is true of human society. Once again there is great diversity and change. But there are also patterns to human life and limits beyond which, for example, evil does not seem permitted to go. Pink argues along such lines in his study of God's sovereignty:

> _For the sake of argument we will say that every man enters this world endowed with a will that is absolutely free, and that it is impossible to compel or even coerce him without destroying his freedom. Let us say that every man possesses a knowledge of right and wrong, that he has the power to choose between them, and that he is left entirely free to make his own choice and go his own way. Then what? Then it follows that man is sovereign, for he does as he pleases and is the architect of his own future. But in such a case we can have no assurance that ere long every man will reject the good and choose the evil. In such a case we have no guaranty against the entire human race committing moral suicide. Let all divine restraints be removed and man be left absolutely free, and all ethical distinctions would immediately disappear, the spirit of barbarism would prevail universally, and pandemonium would reign supreme._ [1]

But that does not happen. And the reason it does not happen is that God does not leave his creatures to the exercise of an absolute autonomy. They are free, yet within limits. Moreover, God in his perfect freedom also intervenes directly, as he chooses, to order their wills and actions.

The book of Proverbs contains many verses on this theme. Proverbs 16:1 says that although an individual may debate with himself about what he will say, it is the Lord who determines what he actually speaks: "The plans of the mind belong to man, but the answer of the tongue is from the LORD." Proverbs 21:1 applies the same principle to human affections, using the dispositions of the king as an example. "The king's heart is a stream of water in the hand of the LORD; he turns it wherever he will." Actions are also under the sphere of God's providence. "A man's mind plans his way, but the LORD directs his steps" (Prov. 16:9). So is the outcome. "Many are the plans in the mind of a man, but it is the purpose of the LORD that will be established" (Prov. 19:21). Proverbs 21:30 sums up by saying, "No wisdom, no understanding, no counsel, can avail against the LORD."

In the same way, God also exercises his rule over the spirit world. The angels are subject to his express command and rejoice to do his bidding. The demons, while in rebellion against him, are still subject to God's decrees and restraining hand. Satan was unable to touch God's servant Job until God gave his permission, and even then certain bounds were set: "Behold, all that he has is in your power; only upon himself do not put forth your hand" (Job 1:12); "Behold, he is in your power; only spare his life" (Job 2:6).

Playing by God's Rules
The point of major interest for us is not in the area of God's rule over nature or the angels, however. It is how God's providence operates with human beings, particularly when we decide to disobey him.

There is, of course, no problem at all with the providence of God in human affairs if we obey him. God simply declares what he wants done, and it is done—willingly. But what about those time when we disobey? And what about the great number of unregenerate people who apparently never obey God willingly? Does God say, "Well, I love you in spite of your disobedience, and I certainly don't want to insist on anything unpleasant; we'll just forget about my desires"? God does not operate in that fashion. If he did, he would not be sovereign. On the other hand, God does not always say, "You *are* going to do it; therefore, I will smash you down so you have to!" What does happen when we decide we don't want to do what he wants us to do?

The basic answer is that God has established laws to govern disobedience and sin, just as he has established laws to govern the physical world. When people sin, they usually think that they are going to do so on their own terms. But God says, in effect, "When you disobey, it is going to be according to my laws rather than your own."

We see a broadly stated example in the first chapter of Romans. After having described how the natural man won't acknowledge God as the true God or worship him and be thankful to him as the Creator, Paul shows that such a person is thereby launched on a path that leads away from God which causes him to suffer grim consequences, including the debasement of his own being. "Claiming to be wise, they became fools, and exchanged the glory of the immortal God for images resembling mortal man or birds or animals or reptiles" (Rom. 1:22-23).

Then comes a most interesting part of the chapter. Three times in the verses which follow we read that because of their rebellion "God gave them up." Terrible words. But when it says that God gave them up, it doesn't say that God gave them up to nothing, as if he merely removed his hand from them and allowed them to drift away. In each case it says that God gave them up *to* something: in the first case, "to impurity, to the dishonoring of their bodies" (v. 24); in the second case, "to dishonorable passions" (v. 26); and in the third case, "to a base mind and to improper conduct" (v. 28). In other words, God will permit the ungodly to go their own way, but he has determined in his wisdom that when they go, it will be according to his rules rather than their own.

If anger and tension go unchecked, they produce ulcers or

high blood pressure. Profligacy is a path to broken lives and venereal disease. Pride will be self-destructive. These spiritual laws are the equivalent of the laws of science in the physical creation.

The principle is true for unbelievers, but it is also true for believers. The Old Testament story of Jonah teaches that a believer can disobey God, in fact, with such determination that it takes a direct intervention by God in history to turn him around. But when he does he suffers the consequences that God has previously established to govern disobedience. Jonah had been given a commission to take a message of judgment to Nineveh. It was similar to the great commission that has been given to all Christians, for he was told to "Arise, go to Nineveh, that great city, and cry against it; for their wickedness has come up before me" (Jon. 1:2). But Jonah didn't want to do God's bidding, as Christians today often don't. So he went in the other direction, taking a ship from Joppa, on the coast of Palestine, to Tarshish, which was probably on the coast of Spain. Did Jonah succeed? Not at all. We know what happened to him. He ran into trouble as God took drastic measures to turn him around. After God let him sit in the belly of a great fish for three days, Jonah decided he would obey God and be his missionary.

The Flow of History
Thus far, our study has revealed several uniquely Christian attitudes toward providence. First, the Christian doctrine is personal and moral rather than abstract and amoral. That makes it entirely different from the pagan idea of fate. Second, providence is a specific operation. In Jonah's case it dealt with a particular man, ship, fish and revelation of the divine will in the call to Nineveh.

There is something else that must be said about the providence of God It is *purposive;* that is, it is directed to an end. There is such a thing as real history. The flow of human events is going somewhere as opposed to being merely static or without meaning. In Jonah's case, the flow of history led to his own eventual, though reluctant, missionary work and then to the conversion of the people of Nineveh. In the larger picture, history flows on to the glorification of God in all his attributes, primarily in the person of his Son, the Lord Jesus Christ. That idea is captured in the definition of providence found in the Westminster Confession of Faith which reads, "God the great Creator of all things doth uphold, direct, dispose, and govern all creatures, actions, and things, from the greatest even to the least by His most wise and holy providence, according to His infallible foreknowledge, and the free and immutable counsel of His own will, _to the praise of the glory of His wisdom, power, justice, goodness, and mercy_" (5, i).

The flow of history leading to the glorification of God is to our good also. For "we know that in everything God works for good with those who love him, who are called according to his purpose" (Rom. 8:28). What is our good? Obviously, there are many "goods" to be enjoyed now, and this verse includes them. But in its fullest sense our good is to enter into the destiny we were created for: to be conformed to the image of Jesus Christ and thus "to glorify God, and to enjoy him forever." The providence of God will surely bring us there.

To speak of the "good" introduces the subject of the "bad." And since the verse in Romans says that "in everything God works for good" to those who are the called ones of God, the question immediately arises as to whether or not this includes the evil. Is evil under God's direction? It would be possible to interpret Romans 8:28 as meaning that all things _consistent with righteousness_ work to good for those who love God, but in the light of Scripture as a whole that would be an unjustified watering down of the text. It is _all_ things, including evil, that God uses in accomplishing his good purposes in the world.

There are two areas in which God's use of evil for good must be considered. First, there is the evil of _others_. Does this work for the believer's good? The Bible answers Yes by many examples. When Naomi's son, an Israelite, married Ruth, a Moabitess, the marriage was contrary to the revealed will of God and hence was sin. Jews were not to marry Gentiles. Still the marriage made Ruth a daughter-in-law of Naomi and thus enabled her to be exposed to the true God and eventually come to the place where she made a choice to serve him. "Your people shall be my people, and your God my God" (Ruth 1: 16). After Ruth's husband died, she married Boaz. Through her new husband Ruth entered into the line of descent of the Lord Jesus Christ, the Messiah (Mt. 1:5).

David was a person who undoubtedly suffered greatly through the sins of others against him, including even the sins of his sons. But as God worked in him through these experiences he grew to see the hand of God in his suffering and expressed his faith in great psalms. The psalms have been an immeasurable blessing to millions.

Hosea suffered through the unfaithfulness of his wife Gomer. But God used his experience to bring forth one of the most beautiful, moving and instructive books of the Old Testament.

By far the greatest example of the sin of others working for the good of God's people is the sin which poured itself out against the Lord Jesus Christ. The leaders of Christ's day hated him for his holiness and wished to eliminate his presence from their lives. Satan worked through their hatred to strike back at God by encouraging merciless treatment of the incarnate Christ. But God turned this to good, working through the crucifixion of the Lord for our salvation. In none of this was God responsible for evil, though human sin and the sin of Satan were involved. In none of this was God made a partner in sin. Jesus himself said, in reference to Judas, "The Son of man goes as it is written of him, but woe to that man by whom the Son of man is betrayed!" (Mt. 26:24). Earlier he had said, "It is necessary that temptations come, but woe to the man by whom the temptation comes!" (Mt. 18:7). Neverthe-less, without himself being a party to sin, God worked through it to bring forth good in line with his own eternal purposes.

The other area in which God's use of evil for his own pur-poses must be considered is *our own sin.* This point is some-what harder to see, for sin also works to our own unhappiness and blinds our eyes to God's dealing. But there is good in-volved anyway. For example, Joseph's brothers were jealous of him because he was their father's favorite. So they con-spired and sold him to a group of Midianite traders who took him to Egypt. There Joseph worked as a slave. In time he was thrown into prison through the unjust accusations of a re-jected woman. Later he was brought to power as second only to Pharaoh and became the means by which grain was stored during seven years of prosperity for the subsequent seven years of famine and widespread starvation. During that period his brothers, who were starving along with everyone else, came to Egypt and were helped by Joseph.

They were helped by the one they had rejected! And the outcome was in God's control, as Joseph later explained to them.

> *I am your brother, Joseph, whom you sold into Egypt. And now do not be distressed, or angry with yourselves, because you sold me here; for God sent me before you to preserve life. For the famine has been in the land these two years; and there are yet five years in which there will be neither plowing nor harvest. And God sent me before you to preserve for you a remnant on earth, and to keep alive for you many survivors. So it was not you who sent me here, but God."* (Gen. 45:4-8)

After the death of their father, the brothers thought that Joseph would then take vengeance on them. But he again calmed their fears saying, "Fear not, for am I in the place of God? As for you, you meant evil against me; but God meant it for good, to bring it about that many people should be kept alive, as they are today" (Gen. 50:19-20). There had been great evil in the hearts of the brothers. But God used their evil, not only to save others, but even to save their own lives and those of their wives and children.

Patience and Gratitude

There will always be some who hear such a truth and immediately cry out that it teaches that Christians may sin with impunity. This accusation was made against Paul (Rom. 3:8). But it teaches nothing of the kind. Sin is still sin; it has consequences. Evil is still evil, but God is greater than the evil. That is the point. And he is determined to and will accomplish his purposes in spite of it.

The providence of God does not relieve us of responsibility. God works through means (the integrity, hard work, obedience and faithfulness of Christian people, for example). The providence of God does not relieve us of the need to make wise judgments or to be prudent. On the other hand, it does relieve us of anxiety in God's service. "If God so clothes the grass of the field, which today is alive and tomorrow is thrown into the oven, will he not much more clothe you, O men of little faith?" (Mt. 6:30). Rather than being a cause for self-indulgence, compromise, rebellion or any other sin, the doctrine of providence is actually a sure ground for trust and a spur to faithfulness.

Calvin has left us with wise advice on this subject.

Gratitude of mind for the favorable outcome of things, patience in adversity, and also incredible freedom from worry about the future all necessarily follow upon this knowledge. Therefore whatever shall happen prosperously and according to the desire of his heart, God's servant will attribute wholly to God, whether he feels God's beneficence through the ministry of men, or has been helped by inanimate creatures. For thus he will reason in his mind: surely it is the Lord who has inclined their hearts to me, who has so bound them to me that they should become the instruments of his kindness.[2]

In such a frame of mind the Christian will cease to fret in circumstances and will grow in the love and knowledge of Jesus Christ and of his Father, who has made us and who has planned and accomplished our salvation.

NOTES

Chapter 1
[1]J. I. Packer, *Knowing God* (Downers Grove, Ill.: InterVarsity Press, 1973), p. 32.
[2]Charles Haddon Spurgeon, *The New Park Street Pulpit,* Vol. 1, 1855 (Pasadena, Texas: Pilgrim Publications, 1975), p. 1.

Chapter 2
[1]John Calvin, *Institutes of the Christian Religion,* Vol. 1, ed. John T. McNeill, trans. Ford Lewis Battles (Philadelphia: Westminster, 1960), p. 35.
[2]Os Guinness, *The Dust of Death* (Downers Grove, Ill.: InterVarsity Press, 1973), p. 148.
[3]Calvin, pp. 68-69.
[4]R. C. Sproul, *The Psychology of Atheism* (Minneapolis: Bethany Fellowship, 1974), p. 59.
[5]Sproul, p. 75.

Chapter 3
[1]Calvin, p. 237.
[2]Benjamin Breckinridge Warfield, *The Inspiration and Authority of the Bible,* ed. Samuel G. Craig (London: Marshall, Morgan & Scott, 1959), p. 132.
[3]Ibid., p. 133.
[4]Ibid., p. 299.
[5]Ibid., pp. 299-300.

Chapter 4
[1]Calvin, p. 80.
[2]Ibid., p. 79.
[3]J. I. Packer, " 'Sola Scriptura' in History and Today," in *God's Inerrant Word*, ed. John Warwick Montgomery (Minneapolis: Bethany Fellowship, 1975), pp. 44-45.
[4]Emile Cailliet, *Journey into Light* (Grand Rapids, Mich.: Zondervan, 1968), pp. 11-18.
[5]Calvin, p. 82.
[6]J. B. Phillips, *Ring of Truth: A Translator's Testimony* (New York: Macmillan, 1967), pp. 74-75.
[7]Calvin, pp. 95-96.

Chapter 5
[1]Thomas Watson, *A Body of Divinity: Contained in Sermons upon the Westminster Assembly's Catechism* (1692; rpt. London: The Banner of Truth Trust, 1970), p. 26.
[2]R. A. Torrey, *The Bible and Its Christ* (New York: Fleming H. Revell, 1904-06), p. 26.
[3]F. F. Bruce, *The New Testament Documents: Are They Reliable?* (Downers Grove, Ill.: InterVarsity Press, 1974), p. 82.
[4]Ibid., pp. 82-83.
[5]Torrey, p. 19.
[6]E. Schuyler English, *A Companion to the New Scofield Reference Bible* (New York: Oxford University Press, 1972), p. 26. The author invites the reader also to compare: Mt. 26:21-25 with Ps. 41:9. Mt. 26:31, 56; Mk. 14:50 with Zech. 13:7. Mt. 26:59 with Ps. 35:11. Mt. 26:63; 27:12, 14; Mk. 14:61 with Is. 53:7. Mt. 26:67 with Is. 50:6; 52:14; Mic. 5:1; Zech. 13:7. Mt. 27:9 with Zech. 11:12-13. Mt. 27:27 with Is. 53:8. Mt. 27:34; Mk. 15:36; Jn. 19:29 with Ps. 69:21. Mt. 27:38; Mk. 15:27-28; Lk. 22:37; 23:32 with Is. 53:12. Mt. 27:46; Mk. 15:34 with Ps. 22:1. Mt. 27:60; Mk. 15:46; Lk. 23:53; Jn. 19:41 with Is. 53:9. Lk. 23:34 with Is. 53:12. Jn. 19:28 with Ps. 69:21. Jn. 19:33, 36 with Ps. 34:20. Jn. 19: 34, 37 with Zech. 12:10.
[7]For a fuller discussion of this interesting area of Old Testament studies see Victor Buksbazen, *The Gospel in the Feasts of Israel* (Fort Washington, Pa.: Christian Literature Crusade, 1954) and Norman L. Geisler, *Christ: The Theme of the Bible* (Chicago: Moody Press, 1968), pp. 31-68.
[8]H. A. Ironside, *Random Reminiscences from Fifty Years of Ministry* (New York: Loizeaux Brothers, 1939), pp. 99-107. I have also told this story in *The Gospel of John*, Vol. 1 (Grand Rapids, Mich.: Zondervan, 1975), pp. 226-28.

Chapter 6
[1]Irenaeus, *Against Heresies*, II, xxvii, 2. *The Ante-Nicene Fathers*, Vol. 1, ed. Alexander Roberts and James Donaldson (1885; rpt. Grand Rapids, Mich.: Eerdmans, n.d.), p. 399.

[2]Cyril of Jerusalem, *Catechetical Lectures*, IV, 17. *The Nicene and Post-Nicene Fathers*, Series 2, Vol. 7, ed. Philip Schaff and Henry Wace (1893; rpt. Grand Rapids, Mich.: Eerdmans, n.d.), p. 23.

[3]Augustine, *Epistles*, 82. *The Fathers of the Church*, Vol. 12, "St. Augustine: Letters 1-82," trans. Wilfrid Parsons (Washington, D.C.: The Catholic University of America Press, 1951), pp. 392, 409.

[4]Augustine, "On the Trinity," Preface to ch. 3. *The Nicene and Post-Nicene Fathers*, Series 1, Vol. 3, ed. Philip Shaff (Buffalo: The Christian Literature Company, 1887), p. 56.

[5]J. Theodore Mueller, "Luther's 'Cradle of Christ,' " *Christianity Today*, 24 Oct. 1960, p. 11.

[6]Martin Luther, "Preface to the Old Testament." *What Luther Says: An Anthology*, by Ewald M. Plass, Vol. 1 (St. Louis: Concordia, 1959), p. 71. The passage is quoted in a slightly different translation by Mueller, op. cit.

[7]Martin Luther, "That Doctrines of Men Are to Be Rejected." *What Luther Says: An Anthology*, p. 63.

[8]Martin Luther, *Table Talk*, 44. *A Compend of Luther's Theology*, ed. Hugh Thomson Kerr (Philadelphia: Westminster, 1943), p. 10.

[9]John Calvin, *Calvin's New Testament Commentaries*, Vol. 10, "The Second Epistle of Paul the Apostle to the Corinthians and the Epistles to Timothy, Titus and Philemon," trans. T. A. Small (Grand Rapids, Mich.: Eerdmans, 1964), p. 330.

[10]John Wesley, *A Roman Catechism*, Question 5. *The Works of John Wesley*, Vol. 10 (1872; rpt. Grand Rapids, Mich.: Zondervan, n.d.), p. 90.

[11]Wesley, *Journal*, Wed., July 24, 1776. *The Works of John Wesley*, Vol. 4, p. 82.

[12]W. L. Knox, *Essays Catholic and Critical* (London: Society for Promoting Christian Knowledge, 1931), p. 99.

[13]Clark H. Pinnock, *A Defense of Biblical Infallibility* (Philadelphia: Presbyterian and Reformed, 1967), p. 4.

[14]This classical approach to the defense of Scripture is discussed at length by R. C. Sproul in his essay "The Case for Inerrancy: A Methodological Analysis," in *God's Inerrant Word*, pp. 248-60.

[15]John Warwick Montgomery, "Biblical Inerrancy: What Is at Stake" in *God's Inerrant Word*, p. 33.

[16]Montgomery, p. 36.

[17]Pinnock, p. 8.

[18]"The Bible: The Believers Gain," *Time*, 30 Dec. 1974, p. 41.

Chapter 7

[1]*Encyclopedia of Religion and Ethics*, Vol. 4, ed. James Hastings (New York: Charles Scribner's Sons, 1912), p. 315.

[2]E. C. Blackman, *Biblical Interpretation* (Philadelphia: Westminster, 1957), p. 141.

[3]Emil G. Kraeling, *The Old Testament Since the Reformation* (New York: Harper and Brothers, 1955), p. 94.

4Rudolph Bultmann, *Jesus and the Word* (New York: Charles Scribner's Sons, 1934), p. 8.

5Edgar Krentz, *Biblical Studies Today: A Guide to Current Issues and Trends* (St. Louis: Concordia, 1966), p. 16.

6Portions of the above material on the quest for the historical Jesus and on Bultmann have already appeared in an article by the author entitled "New Vistas in Historical Jesus Research," *Christianity Today*, 15 Mar. 1968, pp. 3-6.

7J. I. Packer, *"Fundamentalism" and the Word of God* (Grand Rapids, Mich.: Eerdmans, 1960), p. 148.

8Ibid.

9*The Common Catechism: A Book of Christian Faith*, eds. Johannes Feiner and Lukas Vischer (New York: The Seabury Press, 1975), p. 101.

10Ernst Kaesemann, *Essays on New Testament Themes* (London: S.C.M. Press, 1964), p. 34.

11Joachim Jeremias, "The Present Position in the Controversy Concerning the Problem of the Historical Jesus," *The Expository Times*, Vol. 69, 1957-58, p. 335.

12Parts of this critique of Bultmann also appeared in "New Vistas in Historical Jesus Research," pp. 3-6.

Chapter 8

1Francis Bacon, "Of Studies," *Essays or Counsels Civil and Moral* in *Selected Writings of Francis Bacon*, ed. Hugh G. Dick (New York: Modern Library, 1955), p. 129.

2Packer, *"Fundamentalism" and the Word of God*, p. 84.

3Frank E. Gaebelein, *Exploring the Bible: A Study of Background and Principles* (Wheaton, Ill.: Van Kampen Press, 1950), p. 134.

4Gaebelein, pp. 138-39.

5Packer, *"Fundamentalism" and the Word of God*, pp. 102-03.

6Martin Luther, *What Luther Says: An Anthology*, Vol. 1, p. 81.

Chapter 9

1Matthew Henry, *Commentary on the Whole Bible*, Vol. 1 (New York: Fleming H. Revell, n.d.), p. 284.

2A. W. Tozer, *The Knowledge of the Holy* (New York: Harper & Row, 1961), p. 34.

3Arthur W. Pink, *The Attributes of God* (Grand Rapids, Mich.: Baker Book House, n.d.), pp. 2-3.

4Tozer, p. 40.

5Ibid., p. 42.

6Pink, p. 41.

7J. I. Packer, *Knowing God*, p. 41.

Chapter 10

1C. S. Lewis, *Mere Christianity* (New York: The Macmillan Company, 1958), p. 33.

2The illustration of the Trinity by light, heat and air is an old one, but

I have borrowed this particular expression of it from Donald Grey Barnhouse, *Man's Ruin* (Grand Rapids, Mich.: Eerdmans, 1952), pp. 64-65.

[3]The way in which Jesus may be said to have "emptied himself" is discussed at greater length by Packer, *Knowing God*, pp. 51-55.

Chapter 11
[1]Arthur W. Pink, *The Sovereignty of God* (Grand Rapids, Mich.: Baker Book House, 1969), p. 263.
[2]R. C. Sproul, p. 139.
[3]Pink, *The Attributes of God*, p. 28.

Chapter 12
[1]Emil Brunner, *The Christian Doctrine of God: Dogmatics*, Vol. 1, trans. Olive Wyon (Philadelphia: Westminster, 1950), p. 157.
[2]Brunner, p. 160.
[3]Tozer, p. 110.

Chapter 13
[1]Pink, *The Attributes of God*, p. 13.
[2]Tozer, p. 63.
[3]Jean Paul Sartre, *No Exit and Three Other Plays* (New York: Vintage Books, 1949), p. 47.
[4]Sproul, pp. 114-16. The entire analysis of nakedness in modern culture is found on pp. 107-18.
[5]Donald Grey Barnhouse, *God's Heirs* (Grand Rapids, Mich.: Eerdmans, 1963), pp. 145-46.

Chapter 14
[1]Brunner, p. 268.
[2]Tozer, p. 59.
[3]Charles Hodge, *Systematic Theology*, Vol. 1 (London: James Clarke & Co., 1960), p. 390.
[4]J. I. Packer, *Knowing God*, p. 70.

Chapter 15
[1]Francis A. Schaeffer, *Genesis in Space and Time* (Downers Grove, Ill.: InterVarsity Press, 1972), p. 33.
[2]Reinhold Niebuhr, *The Nature and Destiny of Man: I, Human Nature* (New York: Charles Scribner's Sons, 1941), pp. 151-52.
[3]Calvin, pp. 186-89; 470-74.
[4]Francis A. Schaeffer, *Death in the City* (Downers Grove, Ill.: InterVarsity Press, 1969), p. 80.
[5]The reference to being made "a little lower than the angels" applies in the first instance to the person of the coming Messiah, the Lord Jesus Christ. But it is in reference to his Incarnation alone that this is said. Therefore, the phrase and, indeed, the entire psalm is also rightly understood as having reference to men and women in general. The following verses refer back to the role of dominion given to Adam and Eve in Genesis: "Thou hast given him dominion over the works of thy

hands; thou hast put all things under his feet" (Ps. 8:6).

[6]John R. W. Stott, *Your Mind Matters: The Place of the Mind in the Christian Life* (Downers Grove, Ill.: InterVarsity Press, 1972), p. 26.

[7]Donald Grey Barnhouse, *Let Me Illustrate* (Westwood, N.J.: Fleming H. Revell, 1967), p. 32; *Teaching the Word of Truth* (Grand Rapids, Mich.: Eerdmans, 1966), pp. 36-37.

Chapter 16

[1]C. S. Lewis, p. 34.

[2]Schaeffer, *Genesis in Space and Time*, p. 21.

[3]Thomas Bethell, "Darwin's Mistake," *Harper's Magazine*, Feb. 1976, pp. 70-75.

[4]Schaeffer, *Genesis in Space and Time*, p. 55.

Chapter 17

[1]Calvin, p. 162.

[2]Ibid., p. 173.

[3]The material on Satan is borrowed in part from chapter fifty-two ("That Other Family," John 8:41-50) of James Montgomery Boice, *The Gospel of John*, Vol. 2 (Grand Rapids, Mich.: Zondervan, 1976).

Chapter 18

[1]Pink, *The Sovereignty of God*, pp. 42-43.

[2]Calvin, pp. 219-20.

SUBJECT INDEX

Aaron, 134
Abraham, 63, 189
Adam, 139, 197, 204; and Eve, 177-78, 195, 199; fall of, 203
Adoption, 147
Ahab, 226
Alcohol, 202
Anabaptist "enthusiasts," 64-65
Ananias, 226-27
Angels, 218-22; assist God's people, 221-22; fallen, 222-25; hierarchy of, 219; ministry of, 220-22; serve God, 220-21; the "elect," 219; value in studying, 219-20
Anger, 233
Anxiety, freedom from, 238-39
Apostles, the, 50
Archaeology, 71
Aristotle, 59
Arius, 143-44
Astruc, Jean, 98
Atheism, psychology of, 32
Atonement, 146
Attributes of God, 125-90; unchangeable, 131
Augustine, Saint, 60, 86, 155, 195; on Scripture, 82
Authority, source of, 53-54
Autonomy, human quest for, 153-55
Bacon, Sir Francis, 111
Balaam, 63
Balak, king, 63
Baptism of Jesus, 146
Barnhouse, Donald Grey, 204
Bauer, Bruno, 101

Baur, Ferdinand Christian, 100
Ben-hadad, 221
Bethell, Thomas, 211
Bethesda, pool of, 71-72
Bible, the, 39-51; accuracy of, 42, 69-73; affects us, 68; alleged errors in, 92-94; an infallible authority, 47; a rock, 94-95; author of, 112; authority of, 42, 53-65; changes lives, 60-61, 76-79; declining views of, 84-86; given through human channels, 115-18; how to interpret, 111-22; human element in, 44-45, 89-91; is God's Word, 40-44, 67, 81; methods of communication, 45-46; "mythology" of, 101-02; one subject of, 61-64; origin of, 68; preservation of, 75; prophecy in, 73-75; responding to, 118-20; result of an "evolutionary" process?, 104-05; superior to other books, 68; taught by the Spirit, 121-22; theme of, 112; truthfulness of, 81-95; trustworthiness of, 88; understands us, 56-58; unity of, 68-69, 112-15; view of in the early Church, 82-84; writers of, 68. See Word of God
Blackman, E. C., 99
Body: death of the, 203-04; importance of the, 197; salvation of the, 204
Body language, 176
Body, soul and spirit, 196-99
Bruce, F. F., 70-71
Brunner, Emil, 10, 161, 164, 185

Bultmann, Rudolf, 87, 101-03, 107-08, 117
Caillet, Emile, 57-58
Calvin, John, 10, 27, 31, 40, 54, 58, 64-65, 83, 86, 89, 197, 219, 238
Camus, Albert, 154
Canon of Scripture, 50
Capital punishment, 200
Celsus, 75
Ceremonies of Israel, 75
Christianity Today, 10
Christ Jesus: and Nicodemus, 15-16; an infallible authority, 88; Bible's subject, the, 61-64; body of, 197; bridegroom, the, 199; deity of, 143-45; glory of, 188-89; historical, the, 10; Lamb of God, the, 114; pre-existence of, 102; resurrection of, 146; Second Coming of, 221; sinlessness of, 102; submitted to Scripture, 48-49; views concerning Scripture, 46-50, 67, 88; wept over Jerusalem, 186
Church, the: bride of Christ, 199; strong, 24
Cicero, 59
Cleopas, 59
Common Catechism, the, 104
Communism, 17
Communist Manifesto, The, 17
Conformity to this world, 24
Council of Trent, 84
Creation, 146; changeableness of, 183-84; flows from God, 210; God's, 193-228; of man, 193-204; of nature, 205-15; of the spirit world, 217-28; orderly, 210; pronounced good